Making Money Out of Thin Air

RANDY W. KIRK and
SHAILA CHAMBERLAIN, CPA | CMA

If you purchase this book without a cover you should be aware that this book may have been stolen property and reported as "unsold and destroyed" to the publisher. In such case, neither the author nor the publisher has received any payment for this "stripped book."

This publication is designed to provide competent and reliable information regarding the subject matter covered. However, it is sold with the understanding that the author and publisher are not engaged in rendering legal, financial, or other professional advice. Laws and practices often vary from state to state and if legal or other expert assistance is required, the services of a professional should be sought. The author and publisher specifically disclaim any liability that is incurred from the use or application of the contents of this book.

ISBN: 9798696158532

Copyright© 2020 by

Randy W. Kirk and Shaila Chamberlain CPA, CMA

All Rights Reserved.

TABLE OF CONTENTS

RANDY'S INTRODUCTION
    What Are The Benefits Of Having Excellent
Financial Records For Your Business 1

SHAILA'S INTRODUCTION
    Thinking Outside The Box……………………….... 19

Chapter 1 – SHAILA
    Assumptions: Why Assume Doesn't
Always Make An A** Out Of U And Me................... 26

Chapter 2 - EFFICIENCIES
    The Road to Wealth Isn't Always More Sales............ 34

Chapter 3 – EMPLOYEE CAPITAL
    Let Your Employees Do The Job You
Hired Them To Do ……………………………….….. 37

Chapter 4 – ASSET EFFICIENCIES
    Let Your Property Work For You…………………..... 50

Chapter 5 – PROCESS EFFICIENCIES
    How To Get From Riverside To New York
Without Stopping In Dallas……………………….….. 60

Chapter 6 – COST BENEFIT ANALYSIS
    Why I'm Five Pounds Heavier And

My Wallet Is Five Pounds Lighter............................ 70

Chapter 7 – ACCOUNTS RECEIVABLE
Are You The World's Worst Banker? 78

Chapter 8 – ACCOUNTING 101
Meets.. The School of Hard Knocks......................... 89

Chapter 9 – DEBT
The Good, The Bad, And The Ugly 135

Chapter 10 – INTERNAL CONTROLS
Keeping What's Yours.. 142

Chapter 11 – COMMON ERRORS
Would You Jump Off A Cliff Just Because Everyone Else Was Doing It?...................... 167

Chapter 12 – RANDY
Margins Matter: How One Small Business Added $100,000 In Profit Through Margin Analysis 176

Chapter 13 – MARGINS MATTER PART 2
Going from $0.00 Personal Income to $100,00 per Year 182

Chapter 14 – FINANCIAL REPORTS REVEAL LUXURIES
A Very Personal Lesson 188

Chapter 15 – FINANCIAL REPORTS REVEAL FANTASY THINKING

What's Your Fantasy? 192

Chapter 16 – KPI

The Six Numbers You
Need To Run Any Business 197

Chapter 17 – WARREN BUFFET

Risk Comes From Not Knowing What You're Doing
Or You Can't Manage What You Don't Count 205

Chapter 18 – COUNT EVERYDAY

The In- N- Out Way 211

Chapter 19 – I INVENTED A WARNING APP

That Was Really Dumb 216

Chapter 20 – DO YOU KNOW WHAT YOUR SALES WERE LAST YEAR

Same Month? The Year Before? 219

Chapter 21 – SERIOUSLY

Where Did All My Cash Go? 225

Chapter 22 – SHAILA

Why Choosing A Great Bookkeeper /
Accountant / CPA Matters 230

Chapter 23 – RANDY

How Much Should I Charge: Various Methods
For Establishing Pricing 238

Chapter 24 – GETTING TO REAL COSTS
    Many Surprises Here **249**

Chapter 25 – INCREASING SALES THROUGH ACCOUNTING

    Seriously!!! **257**

Chapter 26 – FIRING CLIENTS THRU ACCOUNTING
    Hard Choices **268**

Chapter 27 – LITTLE THINGS MATTER
    Why Great Managers Matter **272**

Chapter 28 – FINANCIAL STATEMENTS
    Key To Getting Best Price **278**

A FINAL WORD **284**

RANDY'S INTRODUCTION

What Are the Benefits of Having Excellent Financial Records for Your Business?

Allow me to begin by attempting to read your mind. Think about the headline above. What thoughts occur to you?

"I know there are benefits, but I still have not taken the time to do it."

"It's is not clear to me that the time and expense are worth it."

"I worry that I'll pay too much in taxes if my books are done 100% above board"

"I know almost nothing about bookkeeping or accounting, so I don't really know."

"My books are in great shape, and the benefits are crystal clear. But tell me more."

"My business checking account has money in it, I must be doing fine."

"My CPA takes care of all that."

Did we capture your thoughts about your business in the above quotes? Shaila Chamberlain and I have actually heard these very statements from our clients and friends.

Shaila is a CPA. I asked her to co-author this book because of my deep admiration for her intellect and her approach to working with her clients. You see, most business owners feel that the money they pay a CPA is a cost, like rent or utilities. But that doesn't need to be the case.

Shaila Chamberlain is also a CMA (Certified Management Accountant) and an MBA. She evaluates your accounting records and provides you with methods to increase sales and profits. Like an MD, she uses your company's vital signs to wipe out the bad stuff in your company and provide you with the regimens you need to get more from the analysis than just getting well, but rather move towards having the best health ever.

Her goal with each client is to increase their profits by more than the investment in her services. An ROI for CPA services. Who'd have thunk it?

Now that you know why I asked Shaila to add her deep expertise and experience to this book, let's look deeper at the above responses to the question posed at the outset of this introduction: "What Are the Benefits of Having Excellent Books for Your Business?" Admittedly, it is possible to run a business even if you're "letting your CPA handle it," or "just aren't taking the time." In fact, in Shaila and my experience the vast majority of small business owners are paying little or no attention to their books other than the tax consequences. But what if your attitude was the same across other functions of the business:

"Quality products? Ours have been good enough so far."

"Good customer service? I don't know if ours is good or not."

"Training? Hiring? Employee motivation? We don't need systems for those things."

"Equipment maintenance, computer reliability. It's been okay."

"Advertising ROI. No idea. We buy our ads and hope for the best."

You would be right in assuming that we've heard those comments, too, but most companies do have their eye on the ball with regard to some or all of those areas. It isn't surprising that a company with great products might get by with poor customer service. The client may feel that they have a great product regardless of horrible customer service. It is also possible for a company with great employees to sell so-so products, as some clients are happy to have fast, well trained, friendly folks to deal with, if the cost or quality of the final product or service is not the main concern.

Truly, most companies are not in a position to "do it all." There just isn't time in the day or needed income to pay for every possible improvement in every department that might be made.

Here is the big BUT! There is plenty of money and time to make any improvements if the ROI (return on investment) is high enough.

If you knew that your products were failing 10% of the time, and that as a result you were spending $1,000 per month for rework, customer complaints, freight for returns, bookkeeping for processing returns, and you knew that you could cut those problems by 90% if you spent $1,000 today, you'd be foolish not to do so. If the loss was $100 a month and the cost to fix it was $10,000, very few would make that investment, unless the brand was suffering and there were also expected hidden costs

(hard to get new clients, hard to get existing clients to buy more, etc.)

This is the way it is with bookkeeping and financial reporting. Some of the ROI is obvious and you can make an easy decision. Some is harder to see. And some is insidious and takes its toll over months or years.

But here is the key takeaway we hope that business owners will acquire through reading this book –

Paying for excellent bookkeeping and financial reporting is a PROFIT CENTER, NOT an EXPENSE if the books are properly prepared and analyzed.

Here are 15 of the most important issues that have the potential for huge returns on investment through the use of proper accounting.

1. Accurately tracking sales – Does this seem only too obvious? Hopefully you've never failed to invoice someone or invoiced them incorrectly, but my guess is that this has happened. Good order entry, invoicing, POS systems, and analysis of the reports generated from these systems can spot those kinds of mistakes and also shrinkage due to employee theft.

2. Determining cost of sales – This is a big one, and often makes the cost of bookkeeping into a profit center all by itself. Do you know your cost of sales? Do you know it only as an average or do you know it by product, department, service type, overhead application, and also net of returns, commissions, deals, etc. I (Randy) have saved clients huge amounts of money just by adjusting margins, commissions, and discounting.

3. Determining fixed overhead – You can have great sales and great margins but lose it all due to fixed overhead that has gotten out of control. I have personal experience with this factor.

4. Determining variable overhead – Some expenses go up or down as sales increase or decrease. Are variable overhead numbers being reviewed as your company grows or shrinks?

5. Finding the break-even point – It is very helpful for every company to know its break-even point. When sales are off (due to recession, seasonality, loss of lines, loss of major clients) this metric helps you make quick decisions on lowering costs.

6. Planning of all kinds – Creating great books is step one to good planning. Once you've got some historical numbers, you can now begin to play with the impact of future changes in sales, margins, overhead, markets, products, services, or other strategies.

7. Budgeting – One part of planning is budgeting. It goes without saying that a creating a budget starts with knowing what you currently spend. A budget will then allow you to stay within plan.

8. Reviewing actual results against budget – As noted in #7, good books and fast reporting will allow you to check your progress against all aspects of the budget, then adjust.
9. Determining Key Performance Indicators (KPI) – You should be able to determine a handful of specific metrics that you want to see daily, weekly, or monthly. Those metrics will be early warning systems and/or reasons for jubilation.
10. Tax issues – Most businesses would consider this to be #1. They want their books to be a tool for tax avoidance. However, the truth is this: if you make $60,000 a year and avoid paying taxes on $20,000 of that, your savings will be minimal. If, on the other hand, a great understanding of your books allows you make $120,000 a year and pay all taxes due, you'll be so much better off.
11. Owner's compensation – This could be #1, of course. But if you mind the first ten, this one is much more

likely to be where you want it to be. And if it isn't, you should be able to figure out how to increase sales and/or margins, and decrease costs, overhead, etc., in order to get a great take home amount.

12. Cash flow analysis – A great cash flow analysis is a huge help in avoiding sleepless nights. An accurate cash flow analysis needs to have great books, really great books. Even then, it is a complicated formula to create and customize to your business. A good CPA should be able to help you with this. Wouldn't you love being able to project when you will have cash shortfalls, so that you can find solutions well in advance?

13. Proving your worth to a bank or investor – If you decide that you need to borrow money from a bank or other financial institution, your books will be instrumental in determining: how much you can borrow; the interest rate you'll pay; the type of collateral, both business and personal, you'll need to provide; and the type of reporting you'll be asked to submit on a regular basis.

The better the books, the better the loan provisions for you.

14. When you want to sell all or part of your business – Investors or buyers of your business will also pay more for a company where the assets, liabilities, and income stream are clear and concisely presented.

15. Grants for non-profits – If you are a non-profit or charitable organization hoping to get grants, and/or required by regulations to provide financials, the better they look, the more likely you are to achieve your goals.

If that list didn't convince you to spend way more time and attention to collecting bookkeeping information and creating systems for analyzing that data, I hope the details that follow will move the needle. Let's start with a case study:

Small Business Owner's Grade Card – Financial Statements

It goes without saying that not everyone loves to get their grades. Some fear failure. Psychologists report that some fear success. However, the vast majority of humans are looking for the feedback, affirmation, or challenges that accompany a report on their progress.

In the small business world, we have many grade cards. Some base their success or failure on how often the phone rings, or how crowded the store is. Some look at the daily sales tally or whether the bank account is growing. I've known owners who feel successful when they have a building full of inventory, shiny new machines, or an office humming with employee activity.

While each of these metrics might suggest some measure of the health of the company, each is sadly lacking and potentially misleading.

The beach cruiser business started in Newport Beach, CA, when old Schwinn Cruiser Bikes started being dragged out of storage, given a bit of paint and a dab of grease, to begin life again as a fad. One shop in Newport Beach became a Mecca for the new concept, and within a very short period of time would have scored great grades on every one of the subjects above. The phone was ringing, as was the cash register. The door was busting down with customers, and the employee count and inventory was ever growing.

As sales boomed, bicycle industry suppliers were lined up waiting for a chance to sell goods and services that would help to grow the business even more. In the early days, the shop paid all bills on time or even took their discounts. The suppliers were only too happy to increase the lines of credit, and to even extend longer terms.

Sometimes what seems too good to be true, really is too good to be true. Even as sales continued to be outstanding and increasing, the shop suddenly declared bankruptcy. Many in the industry believed that the owners had siphoned off the money and cheated the suppliers. The truth was much worse. The owners had ended up with nothing to show for their hard work.

What really happened in this case, like so many others, was a failure to exercise good business principles. The accounting was messy. The reporting was incomplete. And no one paid any attention to the financial results. Had they spent even a few hours evaluating the financial information, they would have seen that the business LOSSES were being covered by the PAYABLES. When they closed their doors, they owed their suppliers over $2,000,000.

The financial reports, even though based on sloppy accounting, still would have shown inadequate sales margins, employee overhead outstripping profits, and theft losses by both customers and employees. Most of all they would have shown losses, and that the losses were being covered by increasing payables.

We are coming to the end of the year as this is written. Are you providing your accounting team with good financial information? Is this financial information being correctly allocated to the appropriate general ledger accounts? Are reports being generated in time for you to be responsive? Are you or someone on your team reading, analyzing, and reacting to those financial statements? Will your year-end grade card give you the right information you need to optimize your future?

When you approach an outside CPA, you will want the following:

Profit And Loss Statement (Aka, Income Statement) – You want this to be created with your industry in mind. There are likely to be industry specific income statement guidelines provided by your association. You want a flash statement by the 5th-10th day of the month. This will not be the final, detailed report, but will give you a quick look at the previous month.

The final report for the month should be done by the 20th. You want time to make decisions. Every day counts if some metric is off.

The final information should be plugged into your budget so that variations can be easily spotted. Now is a good time to adjust future projections as necessary.

Balance sheet – Your balance sheet will indicate where you may be increasing or decreasing assets (inventory, cash, receivables) or liabilities (payables, notes, credit cards) faster or slower than planned. This should accompany the income statement.

Cash flow analysis – Here, you'll see if your cash flow plans were accurate. Slower receivables, increased purchases, or special payment terms to customers might alter your plan.

A/R, A/P, Sales, Inventory reports – There are numerous other reports that should be run, but only if they are going to be used. The CPA and ownership should review these tools and decide which ones can be done by computer and which need to be printed and distributed.

Within these reports are many potential sub reports, such as an over 60-day report on A/R, a dead inventory report, or a scrap report. (That last one is a great story. Wait for it later in the book.)

Notes from the CPA – At the very least your CPA should notate anything that is not in line with historical trends and/or budgets. Better is to ask about any one-time oddball item to determine if it is an anomaly or a change that needs to be considered. Best is to think outside the box and point to even those within budget issues that might lead to improved profits. For instance: sales are hitting budget every month. Profits, too. Would this be a good time to increase margins with a price increase, or increase sales with a promotion, or take a few risks on new products.

One last, quick thought before Shaila takes the ball. This is just in case you aren't convinced that the benefits of good books are worth the time and expense. *I (Randy) found two simple issues in the income statement of a $2.5m business that saved the company $250,000 the next year and kept them from closing their doors.* That story and so much more follow.

SHAILA'S INTRODUCTION

Thinking Outside the Box

One day, Randy and I, and a group of 8 or 10 other business owners were sitting in a Masterminds meeting, brainstorming on ways to help improve our businesses. One of our members explained a challenge he was facing.

William owns a telephone and internet cabling company and he's been in business for well over 20 years. Business, it seems, has had its ups and downs for him: when he has jobs, he has to work like crazy to get them completed to his standards, but then he has no time to network, find more work, or take care of any of the other myriad of details that must be addressed when running a business. But when the jobs are completed, his crew sits around with nothing to do, while he networks, looks for more work and takes care of those myriad of neglected details. A vicious cycle to be sure.

"If you have a crew", somebody asks, "why do you have to *work like crazy* to get them completed? Isn't that *their* job?"

"I have to be there", William responds. "The customer is paying for my expertise. I know where to cut into the walls, which cables to use, where the lines should run. I'm the one who quoted the job, so I know all the particulars of the job. It's too risky to depend on my guys to figure it out without my being there."

"Why don't you take a video?" someone else responds.

At that moment his business, his philosophy and his life changed.

Does that sound too dramatic? Let me explain.

When someone said, "Why don't you take a video?" a lightbulb went on in William's head. I have no idea what that someone had in mind when she offered up this suggestion, but our cabling guy took it to mean this:

When he goes to a prospective customer's business to give a quote, he has no trouble selling the job. He knows exactly what he's doing and he's able to communicate that in such a way that the customer understands that this work is an investment worth taking. He asks if he can go ahead and take measurements. This, he says, helps him with his quote and with mapping out the best plan for the customer. The customer, of course, says *yes* and our cable guy gets all the specs for the job.

"*Now*", William says, "*Now,* I'm going to take a video at the same time I'm measuring. I'll explain everything that needs to be done. I'll use this for quoting, of course, but I can give the crew a copy of the video, too. That way, we can discuss it before they go out, they'll have step by step instructions on what to do, and I can be a phone call away if they need me!" Problem solved.

Not just *problem solved,* but real insight into an idea. Not the "Why don't you take a video?" idea, but a much bigger idea. The idea that business success doesn't have to come from the Harvard Business School, Six Sigma or an expensive consultant. The idea is that sometimes the simplest ideas are the best. The idea that a little creativity goes a long way.

So, this is what they mean by *'Work smarter, not harder'*.

While our cable guy was pondering his "AHA!" moment, I suddenly heard the wheels in my own head starting to turn: What if I could quantify this one decision? What if I could mathematically calculate the financial costs and benefits of this one decision and prove to him that this is a sound business decision? Are there others like him, stuck in habits that worked for them at one time, but no longer make financial sense? Could I use math (geez! What a geek I am!) to truly help business owners understand, analyze and make better financial decisions?

My very own "AHA!" moment!

I know what some of you are thinking: you picked up the book because the title sounds like a sexy read, but now that I've invoked the "M" word, you're not too sure. In junior high, we all learned there are two kinds of people: the ones in the Number Sense club and everybody else. (Guess which ones Randy and I were in? And don't worry if you've never heard of the Number Sense Club; that just means you were super cool in junior high.)

If you've never been into math, it's not your fault. Remember the word problems of childhood? If Train A leaves Albuquerque at 10:22 am travelling at 61.6 miles per hour and Train B leaves at 11:46 am travelling at 73.4 miles per hour, which will arrive in Omaha first? The answer of course is, 'NO ONE CARES'. If I really need to be in Omaha by a certain time, I'll probably just fly anyway. Our schools taught us that there are no practical applications of math and left us wishing that, if we ever did find ourselves on a train to Omaha, a fiery collision would quickly put us out of our misery.

Truthfully, though, we calculate every day: *How much time until this yellow light turns red? How many donuts before loosening my belt? If I use ¾ cup sugar for one batch, how much for 2? How may weeks can I skip mowing before the HOA comes calling? How many shoes should I buy in a BOGO ½ off sale?* We don't think about it, because it's mostly intuitive. It's based on experience and judgement and works on the subliminal level. It gets us through life, mostly unscathed, but let's face it: intuitive math is very often wrong; just ask anyone who's ever bought a $100 pair of cowboy boots and a $10 pair of flip flops on a BOGO sale. *

Intuitive math is all well and good when the stakes are low and the consequences mild, but do you really want to trust your *livelihood* to intuition? Even if your business is doing pretty well, aren't you curious to know where your intuition is serving you and where a little math could help? If that's the case, I encourage you to keep reading. I promise, there's no calculus, very little algebra and the last train to Omaha has already left the station.

>*Author's Note*: Buy One Get One ½ off is a brilliant marketing strategy! If the sign read '25% off, but only if you buy 2!' you probably wouldn't think it was such a great deal. These are likely former Number Sense kids getting back at you for taking their lunch money!

Chapter 1 – SHAILA
ASSUMPTIONS

Why Assume Doesn't Always Make an A** out of U and Me

No doubt you've heard that great book title, *Almost everything I need to know I learned in kindergarten.* I'm from Texas, so I have a slightly different take: *Almost everything I need to know I learned from a country saying.*

No white shoes after labor day, if it ain't broke-don't fix it, nobody ever drowned in sweat, don't count your chickens before they hatch, and one of my favorites, don't assume, it makes an A** out of U and Me.

Several years ago, I was with my young daughters at a mommy play group. I was telling the group about a new job I'd just started as an adjunct teacher at a local university.

One of the other moms thought this was great and asked for information because it was just the type of work she was looking for. I told her, in the nicest way possible, that I'd get the information, but that I was pretty sure they required a master's degree. She looked at me and said, "I have a PhD in molecular biology. Do you think they'll accept that?"

Leave your assumptions at the door

That's how I'd like the reader to approach this book. Some of you may have been in business for a while. Everything your business is and does is for a reason. Those reasons could be because you've found the most effective way to run your organization, or it could be that much of what you've created happened organically, out of expediency. Some things you do are out of habit or because you've heard it's what people in your industry do. Whatever the reason you have taken various approaches, whatever you're doing should be questioned. Don't assume that because something worked last year or last decade, that it's still the best way going forward. Don't assume that because something didn't work the first time, that it won't work today. Don't assume that what "everybody else is doing" is right, and don't assume that everything we say in this book will work for you.

You are a business owner. You have the authority, the right, the opportunity to try new approaches, to do things your own way and to look at things from a fresh perspective. I challenge you to really think about your business and question the reasons that you do things the way you do.

It may be that some small changes may lead to some huge leaps in your business, if you're willing to challenge your assumptions and try something new.

That being said, our lives are filled with assumptions that work for us. We won't make it to work on time if we don't assume the alarm will go off, traffic will be bad and the line at

Starbucks will be long. We have to make some assumptions if we are going to navigate life. The trick to assumptions, then, is that they should be made with some basis in the real world, they should always be questioned, and they should be disclosed.

I, too, have my same assumptions about you, the reader. My big assumption for everything that follows, is that your books are in order. If your bookkeeping is sloppy, there is little that can be gained from reading a book that uses your accounting data as the basis for decision making. If we are going to analyze your debt, for instance, but you've booked the liability into a revenue account, your debt analysis is going to be worthless.

As the saying goes: garbage in, garbage out (not a Texas saying).

How do you know if your books are in order? Here are a few quick tests:

- Are you reconciling? Every bank account, every credit card statement, every loan should be reconciled each month. Look at the reconciliation reports. Are there 'uncleared' items that are over a week or two old? Checks sometimes take a month or two to clear, but credit card transactions, EFTs and deposits clear the bank almost immediately. If there is anything still hanging in there from 2018, I can promise you, there are errors that need to be addressed.
- Run a balance sheet as of the last day of last month. Are there any negative balances? There are a few accounts on the balance sheet that typically have negative balances (not really negative, but *contra* accounts, ie asset accounts with credit balances): eg. accumulated depreciation, allowance for doubtful accounts, shareholder distributions. But most accounts should be positive balances. Negative balances in other

balance sheet accounts (cash, accounts receivable, accounts payable, fixed assets, other debt) are usually an indication that you have bookkeeping errors.

- Run an accounts receivable aging report as of today. Is it complete? Are there others who owe your business money, but not included? Are there old bills that have been received, but still show up? Are there negative balances? If any of these problems exist, then the A/R aging report does not accurately reflect the true uncollected receivables owed to you. This is a sure sign that your bookkeeping needs work.

- Run an accounts payable aging report as of today. Is it complete? Are there outstanding invoices showing that you've already paid? Any negative balances? There are always exceptions, but these types of problems usually point to bookkeeping errors that need to be corrected before going forward.

- Run a year to date income statement with month to month comparisons. Are your consistent revenues and expenses being recorded in the same accounts each month? Are there accounts with negative balances?

This is obviously not an exhaustive list. If your books pass all of these tests, I ABSOLUTELY AM NOT giving you any assurance that your books are in order. One thing you should know up front, assurance is a tricky business with accountants. We never, ever give absolute assurance of anything! Sometimes we give *reasonable* assurance or *limited* assurance. If you want assurance, go talk to an accountant on setting up this type of engagement.

This book, again, gives ABSOLUTELY NO ASSURANCE that your financial statements are in order or can be depended upon for any purpose. I am only including these tests as a jumping off point to the rest of the text.

If, however, you fail some or all of these tests, you should run, don't walk, to a qualified accountant. If you don't have one, you can contact me at Shaila@SChamberlainCPA.com

Other Assumptions:

Every math problem has assumptions. We all understand that if the assumptions are incorrect, the calculated answer will very likely be incorrect. In the following pages, we will illustrate many case studies and examples. All of these will have certain assumptions. We will state these assumptions up front, but our assumptions may be nothing like your real-world life. You will have to build your own mathematical formulas using your own calculations and your own variables. Your calculations may lead you to very different solutions than we found and that's ok. The point of this book is not to claim that we've found the answers, it is to show that there are answers to be found when accounting, math and creativity come together.

Chapter 2
EFFICIENCIES

The Road to Wealth Isn't Always More Sales

What is the key to making more money? If you said, "increase sales", you might be right. But you may NOT be right, too. Increasing sales is the world's answer to making more money, but it's only the right answer part of the time.

The Income Statement is made up of several components, revenues (or sales) being only one part. Many, many variables come together to determine the profitability of a company, including the cost of labor and materials, salaries, administrative and selling costs, rent and the cost of capital. Changes in any one of these areas can lead to greater profitability, yet most of us will concentrate the largest part of our efforts into increasing one component: revenue.

Why is this? Higher revenues will bring in more money, to be sure. It will also increase labor costs, time and effort expended and material usage. It means more customers, more customer service, more billing, collecting, bookkeeping and headaches. We think of increasing sales as the "easiest" way of increasing profitability, but when you really think about it, there is nothing "easy" about it. What if you didn't look to the "easy" answer of more sales, and instead looked for a more creative way to become profitable?

A Better Answer Is To Use Your Resources In The Most Efficient Way Possible.

At this very moment, you probably have hundreds of resources at your disposal. You have your own time, your own knowledge and expertise, your employee's time, knowledge and expertise, some cash in the bank, equipment, furniture, computers, software, Internet, friends, colleagues, books, newspapers, an office, and the list goes on and on. Each one of your resources has utility; it has usefulness to you in some manner or another. Think about your own list of resources for a moment and think about the utility of each one. Are all your resources being used to their maximum utility? What would your business look like if they were?

Efficiency Is About Using Your Resources To Their Maximum Utility To Reach Specific Goals.
Maximizing the utility of your resources will lead to greater profitability with less effort. Intuitively you know this. When you see your employees on their phones in the middle of the workday, you know intuitively that this is costing you money. You may not be able to put your finger on exactly *how* this costs money, but you *know* somehow that you would be better off financially if they were using their time more wisely.

Let's take a closer look at efficiencies and how managing your resources can lead to greater profitability.

Chapter 3
EMPLOYEE CAPITAL

Let Your Employees Do the Job You Hired Them to Do

Employee capital is one of the largest investments most companies make. Hourly wages, overtime, benefits and salaries can cost a company an average of 10-40% of sales. For every $100 in revenues earned, $10 to $40 will be spent on employee capital. For this reason, creating efficiencies in your work force can be a key factor in boosting income.

How do you increase the efficiency of your work force? You increase the utility of each person involved. In order to maximize the efficiency and the utility of your work force, you must assign tasks to the lowest paid, capable person on your staff. For example, you may have several people working in your business and every single one of them is capable of making copies. In fact, your best, brightest, most highly paid and capable employee makes faster copies than anyone on the team.

Does this mean that all copy duties should be given to this employee? Of course not. The copies should be made by the lowest paid, capable person you have. Since anyone in your office can make copies, this job should be tasked to your lowest paid employee. Some people are very good at many, many things. In order to maximize the utility of these individuals, reserve them for the jobs that require their particular expertise.

Are you ready for your first math problem? Let's look at how maximizing the utility of employees at an accounting firm can lead to greater profits:

> Let's say you run an accounting firm and you have 4 employees: Bob, Beth, Bryan and Barb.
>
> Bob is a partner making $250k per year.

Beth is a manager making $160k per year.

Bryan is a staff accountant making $80k per year.

Barb is the office manager making $20 per hour.

The firm's policy is "all-hands-on-deck" during tax season. Everyone (except Barb) prepares returns during this time. Here is the process: make copies, prepare return, review return. Only the partner and manager can review returns, and no one can review their own. Further assume there are 600 returns to be prepared. Tax returns are billed at $300 each.

Employee	Billing Rate	Hourly Pay	Hours to Prepare	Hours to Review	Hours to Copy
Bob	$ 250.00	$ 120.19	0.75	0.50	0.50
Beth	$ 160.00	$ 76.92	1.00	0.75	0.50
Bryan	$ 80.00	$ 38.46	1.75	---	0.50
Barb	---	$ 20.00	---	---	0.50

If each employee were given an equal number of tax returns to prepare and reviews were split equally and each made his or her own copies, the firm's gross margin would look something

Employee	# to Prepare	# to Review	# to Copy	Hours to Prepare	Hours to Review	Hours to Copy	Revenue Generated	Wages Incurred	Gross Margin by Employee
Bob	200	300	200	150	150	100	$60,000	$48,076	$11,924
Beth	200	300	200	200	225	100	$60,000	$40,383	$19,617
Bryan	200	---	200	350	---	100	$60,000	$17,307	$42,693
Barb	---	---	---	---	---	---	---	---	---
Total	600	600	600	700	375	300	$180,000	$105,766	$74,234

like this:

As you can see from the previous schedule, if the work is split equally, the company makes about $74k during tax season. What happens if making copies is pushed down to the least paid person?

Employee	# to Prepare	# to Review	# to Copy	Hours to Prepare	Hours to Review	Hours to Copy	Revenue Generated	Wages Incurred	Gross Margin by Employee
Bob	200	300	---	150	150	---	$60,000	$36,057	$11,924
Beth	200	300	---	200	225	---	$60,000	$32,691	$19,617
Bryan	200	---	---	350	---	---	$60,000	$13,461	$42,693
Barb	---	---	600	---	---	300	---	$6,000	$(6,000)
Total	600	600	600	700	375	300	$180,000	$88,209	$91,791

In this scenario, Barb is the only one making copies and the firm picks up an additional $18k in profits. The employees with tax expertise are using their time more efficiently and the firm prospers.

If the remaining work requiring the least expertise (preparing returns) is pushed down to the lower paid two workers and the remaining work requiring the most expertise (reviewing) is pushed up to the highest paid, the firm is even more efficient and the firm picks up almost $3k more in profit.

Employee	# to Prepare	# to Review	# to Copy	Hours to Prepare	Hours to Review	Hours to Copy	Revenue Generated	Wages Incurred	Gross Margin by Employee
Bob	---	600	---	---	300	---	---	$36,057	$(36,057)
Beth	300	---	---	300	---	---	$90,000	$23,076	$66,924
Bryan	300	---	---	525	---	---	$90,000	$20,191	$69,809
Barb	---	---	600	---	---	300	---	$6,000	$(6,000)
Total	600	600	600	825	300	300	$180,000	$85,324	$94,676

Now the work is not divided up equally. Bob no longer prepares any tax returns but does all of the review work. The remaining work is split between Beth, the manager and Bryan, the staff accountant. Bryan is the slowest, so he is investing the most time in preparation. He is the lowest paid, most qualified person for the job. Tax work is handled more efficiently than before. Note that even if the firm needs to have Barb work overtime to make all the copies, her overtime rate is $35 per hour, still lower than Bryan's $38.46 per hour. It still makes sense for Barb to make the copies. Only when Barb's hourly rate rises to $26 per hour ($39 overtime rate) does it make economic sense to send her home after 8 hours and let Bryan make his own copies.

What is important to note in all three scenarios, is that the total revenue does not change. The profitability of the tax department increases by about 34% by increasing the utility of its employees without making a single dollar more in sales.

Another great by-product to this example is the learning curve that will inevitably follow. If it takes Bryan an hour and 45 minutes to prepare a return at the beginning of tax season, how long do you think it will take him to prepare a return at the end of the season, after completing 300 returns? I would hazard to guess that if he is able to fully concentrate his efforts in this one area, that his efficiency will skyrocket, making the company even more profitable. I would even predict that Bob and Beth become better and faster reviewers and even Barb will find ways to make copies faster. The following tax season, the team will be so efficient, that they can take on more returns, hire another accountant, Bryan can learn to review, freeing up more of Beth's time to take on higher level work, freeing up Bob's time and so on.

While this strategy makes sense to most people in the abstract, I think it is sometimes difficult to grasp how it works in real life, especially when you are working with fixed costs such as salaries. There are a couple of arguments here:

> *"Salaries are fixed, so I'm paying my employees the same no matter what they do. I might as well have them do what needs to be done right now."*

How many times have you heard this one:

> *"I want to show my employees that I'm not asking them to do anything that I'm not willing to do myself."*

Let's dissect these arguments.

"Salaries are fixed, so I'm paying my employees the same no matter what they do. I might as well have them do what needs to be done right now."

True Statement.

However, this is short-term, all-hands-on-deck, firefighter thinking. Every company has deadlines to meet and will probably need to use their resources in this way some of the time, but it is detrimental to the long-term growth and health of a business. Think about your own employees. Do they all make the same amount of money or are some more highly paid that others? If so, why are they paid more? Presumably, the answer is that the higher paid employee's skills are superior in some way to the others. If that is so, then the skills that employee possesses should be used to the company's advantage.

In our example above, we have to assume that Bob, our partner, has superior skills and more experience than the others, or else he would not be making the big bucks. If we have now freed 100 of his hours, what should he do with them? He should use those skills he's being paid for to maximize the profitability of the firm. For Bob, it may be his ability to bring in clients, so he may choose to increase his networking efforts, or he may be particularly adept at structuring company acquisitions, so he will concentrate his efforts there. Whatever he does with his time, should be geared toward his SPECIFIC strengths, so that he can continue to learn, grow and increase the profitability of the company.

This same principle applies regardless of the company or type of business. It is fine for the floor manager of a manufacturing plant to step in and box up product once or twice to meet a deadline. But understand that this is short-term thinking and doesn't solve a problem; this is firefighting. Your manager's time would be better spent working on processes, training, employee scheduling, etc. to keep problems of this nature from happening in the future. In fact, it could be argued that firefighting is the worst way the manager could spend time. There are more creative ways to get the job done. For example, there may be employees in the shipping department with down time while waiting on the production line to finish boxing the product. Bringing in one of these $20 per hour employees to box product might be a superior solution, or possibly, since boxing is a low-skill job, an office worker making $15 per hour could do the packing; *or even having a staffing company on call to send in workers on an as-needed basis may be a better solution. In this way, the manager's time is freed to perform those specific skills for which his premium salary is meant to cover.

> * **Author's Note:** Some companies operate under a bargaining agreement which may rigidly dictate which employees may work in certain departments or in certain capacities. Also, safety and training are of utmost importance. Employees should be properly trained according to the policies and procedures of any company before working in any capacity. My point is not to give the reader any specific suggestion for implementation, but merely to demonstrate a creative thought process.

"I want to show my employees that I'm not asking them to do anything that I'm not willing to do myself."

This argument goes to the culture of a business. There are many excellent management books that will help a business owner or manager manipulate the culture of an organization; this is not one of them. However, it stands to reason that the way employees interpret management's new "hands off" approach is largely dependent on how management uses its "found" time.

In our accounting firm example, if Bob uses his extra 100 hours to play golf three afternoons a week and have two martini lunches every Tuesday, it is reasonable to expect that his employees will be unhappy, and their work will suffer. They may become less productive and the labor shift will have the opposite of the intended effect.

In our manufacturing example, our manager is paid a premium to manage the production floor and the employees working there. The employees will respect a manager that works towards their best interest, whether he is packing boxes or not. If the manager is spending his days making the environment safe, the machinery running smoothly, solving problems on the floor, creating goals and targets for efficiency, rewarding stellar employees, disciplining problem employees, the workers will be free to perform their jobs efficiently. He doesn't have to be "one of the guys"; he needs to do his job to the best of his ability, in order to improve the quality of his subordinate's working lives and in turn, receive optimal efficiency from his team.

Chapter 4
ASSET EFFICIENCIES

Let Your Property Work for You

For most companies, employees are their biggest resource and also their most challenging resource. However, companies have other assets that should be approached with the same mind set.

Assets, from an accounting perspective, are property that you own that can be used to benefit a current or future period. Some examples of assets are cash, accounts receivable, inventories, machinery and equipment. These things can be used in some way to benefit the company in the current or future periods. Cash can be used to purchase other assets, accounts receivable can be collected or factored (sold for immediate cash to a factoring company) and the money used to pay expenses, inventories might be converted into finished property or sold and so on. In order to receive the highest utility of assets, management should work towards the efficient use of all assets. All other things being equal, assets should be used for their highest intended purpose, when possible.

The people who know me may think that I've always lived the glamorous life of a certified public accountant. Not true! It may surprise you to learn that I once worked in the decidedly *unglamorous* world of envelope manufacturing. The following example was taken from my experience years ago at this facility. I've simplified the variables, somewhat, but the gist of the challenge remains the same:

The plant had 3 envelope making machines with the following capabilities:

> Machine A could only produce #10 envelopes. (For those non-envelope making geeks, a #10 envelope is the most common envelope- 4-1/8" x 10-1/2". It fits an 8-

1/2" x 11" piece of paper when folded.) These types of envelopes are a commodity, meaning that buyers of this product are very price sensitive. They will determine their purchases almost solely by price alone. This particular machine could run almost a million #10 envelopes a day.

Machine B could produce the #10, but also a wide variety of other sizes and types, such as full color direct mail envelopes that contain local business coupons. This machine ran much slower and, depending on the size and style, might run 400 - 500 thousand per day.

Machine C could produce everything Machine B could produce, but also specialty envelopes, such as envelopes with fancy die cuts, offset printing or peel-off adhesive. This machine was very slow and could produce only 20-50 thousand per day.

Special order envelopes (most non-#10s) were not as price sensitive. They were generally made to the specifications of the purchaser, so price was not the only buying consideration. As a rule of thumb, the more intricate the envelope, the higher the selling price, but running costs were also higher for complex products, and there was always more risk of a machine break-down or work-stoppage due to the added complexity of making the product.

In the following example, assume that a company orders 5 million #10 envelopes. Further assume that each machine runs to its capacity, the envelopes sell for $0.05 each and that each machine costs $10k per day to operate.

Since each machine is capable of running #10 envelopes, all machines may be utilized. But is this the most efficient use of resources? The first example displays the total cost and profitability of using all machines in this manner. The order will be shipped to the customer in less than 4 full days, with a profitability of just over $154 thousand.

	Machine A	Machine B	Machine C	Daily Total
Day 1	1,000,000	500,000	50,000	1,550,000
Day 2	1,000,000	500,000	50,000	1,550,000
Day 3	1,000,000	500,000	50,000	1,550,000
Day 4	350,000	---	---	350,000
Total	3,350,000	1,500,000	150,000	5,000,000
	Machine A	Machine B	Machine C	Total
Total Cost	$40,000	$30,000	$30,000	$100,000
Cost / Envelope	$0.0119	$0.0200	$0.2000	$0.2319
Revenue	$167,500	$75,000	$7,500	$250,000
Gross Margin	$137,500	$45,000	$(22,500)	$160,000

In this example, Machine A is the most profitable, returning almost $138 thousand to the bottom line. While the overall run is profitable to the company, Machine C actually *loses* money on the run. It is clearly *not* in the best interest of the company to use Machine C in this manner.

The second example shows what would happen if only Machines A and B ran the order. The job would still finish in day 4 (although slightly later in the day), but profitability is now expected to be $165 thousand, an $11 thousand increase.

	Machine A	Machine B	Machine C	Daily Total
Day 1	1,000,000	500,000	---	1,500,000
Day 2	1,000,000	500,000	---	1,500,000
Day 3	1,000,000	500,000	---	1,500,000
Day 4	334,000	166,000	---	500,000
Total	3,334,000	1,666,000	---	5,000,000
	Machine A	Machine B	Machine C	Total
Total Cost	$40,000	$40,000	---	$80,000
Cost / Envelope	$0.0120	$0.0240	---	$0.0360
Revenue	$166,700	$83,300	---	$250,000
Gross Margin	$126,700	$38,873	---	$165,573

The elimination of Machine C clearly is mathematically, a great decision. But could the machines be run even more efficiently? Could the company make even more money on the same amount of sales?

In the third example, the entire order is produced on machine A. The job would finish in 5 days, rather than 4, but profitability jumps up to $200 thousand, an additional increase of $35k.

	Machine A	Machine B	Machine C	Daily Total
Day 1	1,000,000	---	---	1,000,000
Day 2	1,000,000	---	---	1,000,000
Day 3	1,000,000	---	---	1,000,000
Day 4	1,000,000	---	---	1,000,000
Day 5	1,000,000	---	---	1,000,000
Total	5,000,000	----	----	5,000,000
	Machine A	Machine B	Machine C	Total
Total Cost	$50,000	---	---	$80,000

Cost / Envelope	$0.01	---	---	$0.01
Revenue	$250,000	---	---	$250,000
Gross Margin	200,000	---	---	$200,000

The profitability skyrockets when the machine is utilized at full capacity for its highest intended purpose. The business manager will have to weigh the added profitability against the needs of the customer and its delivery requirements.

Note, again, that the overall sales revenue does not change. The sales amount of the order remains at $250k, but the profitability of the order increases by about 30%, or about $46 thousand.

Additionally, 3 to 4 days are saved on Machines B and C, opening up the possibility of running specialty envelopes on those machines. As you may recall from the example, specialty orders are not as price sensitive as #10s, so we would expect those orders to generate a higher margin, leading to an even greater increase in profitability.

Another area where assets are often inefficiently used is in warehousing. Consider the rental cost of warehousing space: if 10 thousand square feet of warehouse space costs $15k per month to rent, it equates to $1.50 per square foot. If 10% of that space is housing obsolete product, then $1,500 per month, or $18 thousand per year is wasted. That space could be used to hold higher margin, faster-moving product, or a portion of the warehouse could be sublet, or the company may find a smaller, less expensive warehouse. There are several options the company could consider that might make more economic sense than housing product "just in case" a customer might suddenly have a need for it in the future.

All assets, from large machinery, to computers, to cash, to hours in the day, should be carefully considered before committing them to a project out of habit or immediate expediency.

Chapter 5
PROCESS EFFICIENCIES

How to Get from Riverside to New York Without Stopping in Dallas

If I wanted to travel from my house in Riverside California, to New York City, how would I do it? I might fly, drive, take a train (at least some of the way), ride my bike or even walk. If I decide to drive, I might take my own car, rent one, hitchhike, take a cab, carpool or Uber. If I hitchhike, I might get a ride to Palm Springs and then to Phoenix but have to walk through Northern Arizona and so on.

The point is, there are infinite number of ways I can get from Riverside to New York and some will get me there much faster and cheaper than others. The same is true of your business.

Processes are those series of tasks that take a company from Point A to Point B; from raw material to end product; from bill of lading to invoice; from customer complaint to satisfied customer. The question is: Are you hitchhiking or flying? Do you have a layover in Dallas or are you flying direct?

Processes use your resources to get you from Point A to Point B. We've already talked about using those resources in their most efficient way. Process management is a way of using your most valuable resource in its most efficient way.

Take for example a flooring company. Let's assume that Fred's flooring has the following procedure for sales:

1. Potential Customer calls and is interested in purchasing and installation of carpeting and wants an estimate. Fred says that in order to give an estimate, he will need measurements.
2. Fred sends Measurer out to Potential's house, who measures (giving the dimensions to Potential) and advises Potential to visit the showroom for the next step.

3. Potential visits the showroom and picks out carpet, signs the paperwork and the job is scheduled.

What are some inefficiencies in this process?

Fred says that a good percentage of potentials are lost very early in the process. They don't yet know what they want or how much they are willing to pay. Once they have measurements, it's very easy to go to Home Depot or Google and get estimates on their own. Also, their measurement guy is very handy with the tape measurer, but his sales skills are very rudimentary. Fred says that at this early stage in the game, it's easy to scare off Potentials. Therefore, Fred estimates that only about 60% of those measured actually make it to the showroom.

Once in the showroom, Potentials meet with a salesperson. Now that they see this huge selection displayed so beautifully, they may start to think about other options, such as tile or hardwoods. Fred says that not all floors are suitable for all options, or sometimes there are extra steps involved with certain floors. As a result, he commonly must send someone back out to the house to check this out before he can quote on tile, as well as carpet.

After all of this is decided, he can finally quote. Fred says that he has a top-notch sales team and he estimates that, once in the showroom, about 65% of customers will sign a contract and purchase. In the meantime, Fred has sent a person out to the house at least once, possibly twice, with very little to no return on this investment in time and labor.

When asked why the steps are performed in this particular order, Fred isn't entirely sure. He thinks it's because it seems logical that he needs the measurements before he can give an accurate quote. He doesn't want his guy to spend more time there than necessary, so he doesn't have him check to see if the rooms are appropriate for other types of flooring, or to invest any sales training in the measurement guy. But Fred admits that the process has happened rather organically, and he's not really ever put much thought into its efficiency or effectiveness.

When the phone rings at Fred's place of business and a potential customer wants an estimate, what does she really need at this point? Does she really need a measurement, or does she need something else? Fred has admitted that at this stage of the game, many potential customers are still trying to figure out what they want and what they can afford.

Perhaps what potential customers need at this stage of the game is not measurement, but guidance? They've reached out to Fred's top-notch team for guidance through the process. If Fred's sales team can convert 65% of shoppers to a sale and his measurement guy can only get 60% just to the next step, would it make sense to get them to the showroom first? This way, the most customer-orientated people on his staff can educate and guide the customer through the process.

Fred may wonder how he will estimate without having the measurements first. This is a legitimate concern, but like all other business decisions he must make, he should give careful thought to different approaches. If most customers are more interested in guidance than exact numbers, it may be worth trying a different approach. His sales staff can ask questions about décor, maintenance requirements, pets, room traffic, budget, etc. and help customers decide what type of flooring works best for them. They can give the customer a budget range and explain that the exact numbers will be slightly different once measurements are taken. The customer can make a deposit and sign a contract with a price per foot option, rather than a total price option right then.

Let's look at this scenario mathematically. Assume Fred's showroom is fantastic, the sales team is top notch and that they truly do convert 65% of lookers into buyers. Assume that 100 people per month will inquire about flooring and the average contract is worth $10 thousand.

	Measure 1st	Showroom 1st
# of Potential Customers	100	100
# Coming to Store	60	100
# Signing Contracts	39	65
Average Contract	$10,000	$10,000
Sales Revenue	$39,000	$65,000

By changing this step, Fred could increase his revenues by $26 thousand per month.

If Fred finds it absolutely essential to measure first, there are still creative ways to solve his problem of getting more people to the showroom. Perhaps he could train his measurers to sell, or train his sellers to measure? He could have measurers take product samples for the customer to see and feel and experience while the employees are taking measurements. He could send a high-quality video of his sales force featuring some of the most enticing products. He could bring before and after photos of some of his best work. He could charge a nominal fee that would cover his workers cost of measuring should the customer decide he isn't interested after all. He could even have the customers Skype with the sales force while the measurement team is working in the house.

Every step of a process should have at least one criterium: is it necessary for meeting the customer's ultimate need? If not, is it needed? It may still be needed. For instance, it could be a legally mandated step, or required by the bounds of your profession, but the customer's needs should be at the forefront.

Real Life Example of Inefficient Practice

Years ago, I was worked as an auditor. As part of my job I would occasionally ask my clients to substantiate some cash receipts. Many times, I was surprised by clients who would bring me a xerox copy of cash currency they had taken in – actual photocopies of $20 bills. Someone in the past had taught them to take photocopies of checks to substantiate money received in by check and then inferred that if it worked to substantiate checks, it must also work to substantiate cash.

Actually, it doesn't.

If the supervisors in this department had thought about it for a few minutes, they would have realized that check copies show detail that can be used to prove the origination of a payment: the name of the customer, the amount, the check number, the bank it was drawn upon, the date, etc., while copies of cash offer none of this evidence. Cash is extremely generic (except for the serial numbers, but when have you ever known anyone to record serial numbers?). Yet every single day, they were sending employees to the xerox machine to make copies of U.S. currency, never questioning the process or what was achieved in doing so.

Speaking rhetorically, I believe that all businesses have someone "copying the cash". Think of your own business. If you were to analyze each of your employees and the tasks each takes on each day, how many processes would you find that were simply "copying the cash"?

Spend some time on this. Review your company's procedures and weed out everything that is not a benefit to the customer or a matter of legal compliance. Find the smartest way to do things. Imagine where your business could be if every minute that you've paid someone to do something mindless and stupid could be refashioned towards greater efficiency and effectiveness (code for more profitable, less work).

Chapter 6
COST BENEFIT ANALYSIS

Why I'm Five Pounds Heavier and My Wallet Is Five Pounds Lighter

Have you ever bought a gym membership? On January 1st it seems like a great idea! It costs about $30 per month; that's only $1 every time you plan to use it. A screaming deal! You will finally lose that 20 pounds that's been haunting you for years! $1 per day is a small price to pay for such a life-altering opportunity!

Then life happens – you miss a day or two here and there; your knee starts to hurt so you need to take some time off to rehab; work starts overwhelming you; the kid's schedules are crazy, etc. By March, you quit going all together, but you wouldn't think of cancelling the membership. It's only $30 per month and it's there for you when you're ready to start back.

Instead of going every day, you're lucky if you make it twenty times a year! Instead of the gym costing $1 every time you used it, it's actually cost you $18 every time you used it! And the 20 pounds? A year later, you only need to lose 25 pounds!

Personally, this is the biggest cost/benefit fail of my life. I have paid for a gym membership every month of my adult life, and seriously, there have been full YEARS where I didn't darken the doors ONE SINGLE TIME! Who in their right mind would pay $360 per year for the OPPORTUNITY to run on a treadmill? It's purely illogical thinking!

Once upon a time, I worked for a public accounting firm. Every year, the first two weeks of January was a busy time where we frenetically worked to get out the "tax organizer" to our clients. A tax organizer is a document that almost all tax software will kick out that allows an accountant to interview his clients about their previous year's financial activity. It's very helpful for a couple of reasons. First, the organizer asks questions about almost every conceivable taxable event a client might encounter. It helps ensure that we don't miss anything pertinent that could be a taxable event or deduction to the client. Secondly, it serves as a quasi-legal document. Once it's completed, it shows that the accountant did his due diligence and will also offer proof if a client lied about his situation or intentionally misled his accountant.

During January, we printed out an organizer for every active tax client, compared the address printed on the form to physical records to ensure that no address changes had been missed, stuffed them in specialty envelopes, ran them through the postage meter, and drove them to the post office for mailing. All the while, we knew that only a very small percentage of those who received the tax organizer would bring it to their tax meeting, and fewer still would have filled out any portion of it, let alone completed it.

When I started my own firm, I needed to think about the tax organizer and how I would use it. (Having no money really is a big incentive for re-thinking how to get things done!) I put together a little cost/benefit analysis on mailing out the organizer.

Assumptions:

- *1,000 active tax clients receiving an organizer.*
- *Each client requires 15 minutes of handling time to print, check the address, stuff, run through the postage meter and drive to the post office.*
- *We've learned our lesson (see above), our lowest paid person performs this task, at $15 per hour.*
- *Postage is calculated by weight and costs $1.00 per piece.*
- *10% of clients bring the organizer back and it is complete (big assumption, here!)*
    - *saves our accountant (at $40 per hour) one half hour of time.*

- - For all others the accountant will reprint the document and conduct the interview in person.
- Paper costs $0.20 per organizer
- Envelopes cost $0.10 per organizer

To Summarize:

Labor Cost (1,000 x .25 x $15)	$(3,750)
Postage (1,000 x $1)	$(1,000)
Paper (1,000 x $0.20)	$(200)
Envelopes ($1,000 x $0.10)	$(100)
2nd Printing (90% x 1,000 x $0.20)	$(180)
Total Cost	$(5,230)
Labor Saved (10% x 1,000 x $40 x .5)	$2,000
Total Cost to Firm	**$(3,250)**

As you can see from the example, the whole enterprise actually costs the company just over $3 thousand. The costs outweigh the benefits.

Now let's change our analysis and consider emailing our organizers instead.

Assumptions:

- *1,000 active tax clients receiving an organizer.*
- *Each client requires 5 minutes of handling time to download, check the address, and send*
- *We've learned our lesson (see above), our lowest paid person performs this task, at $15 per hour.*
- *10% of clients bring the organizer back and it is complete (We think the same percentage do as they're told regardless of what medium they receive)*
    - *saves our accountant (at $40 per hour) one half hour of time.*
    - *For all others the accountant will reprint the document and conduct the interview in person.*
- *Paper costs $0.20 per organizer*

Labor Cost (1,000 x 5/60 x $15)	$(1,250)
2nd Printing (90% x 1,000 x $0.20)	$(180)
Total Cost	$(1,430)
Labor Saved (10% x 1,000 x $40 x .5)	$2,000
Total Benefit to Firm	**$570**

In this example, the benefits actually outweigh the costs by almost $600, creating an increase in company profits of almost $4 thousand.

Certain variables must be assumed, based on experience or other factors, while others are easily quantifiable. In all decisions, the costs should be weighed against the benefits before committing resources. This does not necessarily mean that the firm should change its practices; there are always intangibles that are difficult to quantify in an analysis. In this example, we cannot quantify some of the benefits.

For example, some clients will receive the organizer and be prompted to call right away for an appointment. The earlier that a client books their appointments, the more opportunity the firm has to plan and organize their resources, thus helping them to operate more efficiently. Some clients may not complete the organizer, but they use it to prompt them to bring the correct documents to the meeting. This will also help the firm to operate more efficiently. Some clients will think that the firm is super-organized or really cares about them, etc., so that helps with client retention and referrals. Keep in mind there may be unquantifiable costs, as well. Cost/benefit analysis is a starting point, but always make sure that the intangibles are considered too.

Chapter 7
ACCOUNTS RECEIVABLE

Are You the World's Worst Banker?

Call me crazy, but I sometimes wonder whether the entire concept of accounts receivable is outdated. In the old days, Pa Farmer approached the merchant at the general store to buy seed to plant crops. He couldn't pay for the seed until the harvest was sold, he would explain to the merchant, but he was good for the money. The merchant was in a bind: he needed to unload the seed, but all of the farmers were broke until spring. The farmers were in a bind: they couldn't make a living without the seed, but wouldn't have any money until the corn was eventually sold. Thus, the accounts receivable was born. The merchant sold the seed to Pa Farmer in exchange for a promise to pay in the future. (I have no idea how the A/R was born. I made up this story to illustrate a point).

Today, money moves fast. There is PayPal and Venmo and Mastercard and bank transfers. If Pa Farmer approached Home Depot today with his lame excuses, they would listen patiently, nod their heads sympathetically, and offer him their very convenient credit card option, with a reasonable 22% interest rate attached. They would not offer up a traditional accounts receivable option.

Let's call Accounts Receivable what it truly is: an interest free loan to your customers. Did you know you were in the banking business? And now that you know it, do you realize that the interest rate you are charging (0%) makes you a very poor banker? In fact, if we were to dive into your books today, I would wager that we would find some credit card debt, a loan or two, and possibly a working capital line of credit. What these things have in common are interest charges. You are paying interest on borrowed money, because you are cash-strapped, in part because you LENT money to your customers. In other words, you BORROWED money from various banks at market interest rates in order to LEND money to your customers for no interest at all!

Does that make sense to you, quite possibly, the world's worst banker?

Complicating this scenario is that A/R, once it has found its way onto your books, very rarely manages itself, does it? Ask yourself how many of your customers or clients pay within the terms of your invoice. It's probably a pretty low percentage. Because once a customer finds an interest-free banker, he'll make you hound him for the payments. You have the time and energy for that, right?

There are a couple of other concepts that we should also touch on briefly:

Opportunity Cost - the loss of the opportunity for potential gain from other alternatives when one alternative is chosen.

When you spend your days (or worse, evenings) trying to collect money you earned two to three months ago, you are missing out on the awesome opportunities that are staring you in the face right now (or would be, if you could look up from the aging report long enough to see them).

Time Value of Money – a dollar today is worth more than it will be tomorrow.

A great example of this principle is the lottery. If you were to win a million dollars in the lottery tomorrow, you might think you are finally a millionaire. Not so fast. To receive the full million, you will be paid an annuity over a 30-year period of just over $33 thousand per year. You would have to save every one of those $33 thousand checks over that 30-year period to be considered a millionaire. While I don't know anyone who would turn down an extra $33 grand a year, I also don't know anyone who could actually quit her job and move to Tahiti, either.

But the lottery also offers a lump-sum cash payment alternative. If you don't want to wait 30 years to become a millionaire, you can take a smaller sum today. Much smaller. Much, much smaller. About 55% to be exact. It turns out, that your million- dollar lottery ticket is only worth about $550 thousand in cash (and, not to be too depressing, but… that's before Uncle Sam takes a bite).

Why is your million dollars only worth $550k today? Because of the time value of money. It's a somewhat complicated math formula that takes into account an estimated return on money if it were invested over time and then converts it back into today's dollars. The lottery managers knows that the farther out in time you go, the cheaper money gets – there are a lot of uncertainties in the future, and they are betting that if they invest $550k today, they will have enough money to make your $33k annual payout over time.

You may be wondering how this relates to your $10 thousand worth of accounts receivable. Well, it's the same concept. Theoretically, if you were to receive $10 thousand cash today, you could invest it in a wide variety of inventories, equipment, product lines, r & d, etc., but tomorrow is uncertain: the stock market could crash, your customer could go out of business, or he just may decide not to pay you. If the $10k is received a year from today, you'd need to receive $10.5k or $11k (depending on expected market returns) to receive the same utility as receiving it today. As the world's worst banker, you've just lost an additional $500 to $1,000.

Remember: money is always worth more to you today than it will ever be in the future. Inherently you know this. That's why if someone offers you a dollar today or a dollar and five cents a year from now, you just know you'd rather have that dollar now.

Both the concept of opportunity cost and the time value of money can be illustrated and proven mathematically. But on page 1 of this book, I promised simple math and I am a person of my word. If you'd like a more in-depth analysis of these concepts and some really meaty math, check out my blog at www.schamberlaincpa.com

Don't worry, you're not alone. Small businesses often work this way. As we've said repeatedly in this book, sometimes there are valid, intangible reasons for the practices we use, and though they don't necessarily make mathematical sense, they are still appropriate for our business. However, it is good to challenge the common wisdom from time to time. If you are accumulating A/R out of habit, without putting any real thought into whether there is a better way, you are probably not operating at your most efficient level. As we've pointed out over and over, Efficiency = Profits.

Even if you forget the time value of money, there is still a cost to running A/R the old-fashioned way. Many of my clients are adamant against taking credit cards as a form of payment, because of the associated costs. It is hard to watch a big chunk of money leave your bank account each month, I agree. However, a good manager does not make a decision based on only half of the information (the cost), but rather a good manager must weigh the costs against the benefits.

Let's look at an example:

ABC, a large service corporation has the following average accounts receivable balance.

ABC finds that about 75% of their customers pay within the first 30 days, 81% pay within the first 60 days, 82% pay in the first 90 days and 18% are over 90 days old. Those that are over 90 days old are sent to a collection department where they are given only 25 cents on the dollar for money received. About 5% of total sales becomes totally uncollectible.

Currently, they do not take credit cards. Many of their clients have asked that they take credit cards as a form of payment.

ABC pays has an employee that calls every client who has not paid according to the following schedule:

    31 – 60 days - every other week

    61 – 90 days – weekly

The employee earns $15 per hour, spending about 5 hours per week on collection work.

ABC estimates that if the company accepted credit cards, about one half of their customers would take advantage of that option and that 90% of their customers would pay within the first 90 days and only 2% would become uncollectible. Further, ABC estimates that the employee would only spend 3 hours per week in following up on past due customers. Assume an average month's sales on account of $50,000 and credit card fees of 3%.

In this example, is there a financial benefit to ABC company accepting credit cards?

	Without Credit Card Option			With Credit Card Option	
Days Outstanding	Pay Rate	Received		Pay Rate	Received
0-30	75%	37,500		85%	42,500
31-60	6%	3,000		4%	2,000
61-90	1%	500		1%	500
91-	13%	6,500		8%	4,000
Uncollectible		2,500			1,000
Total Collectible		47,500			49,000
Employee time per month		(300)			(180)
Payment to collection agency		(4,875)			(2,000)
Credit card fees		-			(750)
Total Collected on $50k sales		42,325			46,070

While many of us ASSUME that accepting credit cards is the more expensive option, in this case the company can expect to be $3,745 more profitable in the month; $44,940 more profitable over the course of a year. In fact, using this same scenario, the credit card company would have to charge 18%

for the company to find its current process the more profitable of the two.

And this example does not even take into account that the employee will now have 2 hours each week freed up to work on making ABC an even more profitable enterprise.

As a final note, credit cards are not the only answer. There are more ways for customers to pay electronically than ever before, and many of those options are much cheaper than average credit card fees. I encourage you to shop around, do the math, and come up with the most cost-effective combination of payment options for your own company.

Chapter 8
ACCOUNTING 101

...Meets...The School of Hard Knocks

You may have noticed from the cover that I have a few letters after my name. From that, you can safely assume that I've spent a fair amount of my life in class and studying. You might assume that such a history would make me somewhat of an expert in my field. Sadly, that didn't happen.

In school, I learned basic accounting concepts: how to correctly book financial transactions, understanding and preparing financial statements, auditing concepts, tax law and other basics of accounting. The real education has taken place through years of working with employers and clients in the application of those theoretical concepts.

For example, my education taught me how to calculate a gross margin, my experience has taught me why we need to, how to dissect it, how to influence it and how influencing it will filter down to the bottom line.

In the previous chapters, we talked about some easy-to-understand concepts that you can use to make improvements in your business. This chapter is more complex. It requires that you understand some of those basic managerial accounting tenets in order to couple them with your own business knowledge, to then drive greater profitability.

Let's Start With The Concept Of Break-Even.

Break-Even is defined as the sales amount a business must reach in any given period of time to have neither a profit or loss: it breaks even. There is a mathematical point for every business where this lies (assuming, sales mix and variable costs remain stable over a period of time). Why is this number important to know? It helps you understand and plan your cash flow and helps in making realistic goals. Once you've learned to master the elements of break-even analysis, you'll be able to manipulate it, lowering the point at which you break even, thereby bringing in more profits per dollar of sale made.

When I ask most small business owners how much revenue they need to break even, most can give me a number that "feels right" to them. This is a good start. Business owners often run their businesses intuitively and have some success, but intuition only gets you so far, especially as the elements get more complex.

In order to calculate breakeven, you'll need to understand some basic accounting concepts:

Direct or Variable Costs – costs that change with every unit produced. If production fluctuates, these costs fluctuate with them. Think of variable costs in this way: if production were doubled tomorrow, which costs would rise dramatically? Consider a manufacturing facility:

- Wages – Labor is one of the largest costs for almost any employer. Wages come in a few forms. There are employees who are paid by the hour to make product; salaried employees who manage floor operations; employees who are paid by the hour, but work in clerical positions; salaried management; and commission-based sales employees. Direct labor is generally the employees who are directly working with and making the product: the line workers, the forklift drivers, the tool and die makers.

- Materials – Purchases of products that are used to build, package, store and ship goods are considered direct costs: raw materials, boxes, packing peanuts and pallets.

- Utilities – Electricity, water and gas costs can vary dramatically, depending on the amount of production on the factory floor. If the factory is on a separate meter, these costs will be considered direct. If the factory and office environment is on the same meter, a portion of utilities should be allotted to overhead.

- Overhead – Costs that do not necessarily vary but are directly related to the cost of making the product. These costs might be taken in total, such as salaries of factory supervisory personnel or allocated as a percentage of total costs, such as electricity or rent.
- Freight – In – Costs associated with shipping raw materials, products for resale, finishing materials, etc. generally vary with production: if production is down, less materials are ordered and less freight costs are incurred.

Fixed Costs – costs that remain the same each month, regardless of sales or production.

- Salaries – Many employees, such as departmental managers, will be paid the same amount each month. Clerical workers, although usually paid an hourly rate, are also considered fixed costs. This is because their pay does not usually vary with the rate of production or sales but may vary based on the inefficiency of the department or other factors.

- Facility Rental – The amount of rent paid is the same each period. As noted above, a portion of rent should be allocated to manufacturing overhead, based on the square footage of area devoted to production.

- Utilities – At first glance, utilities might be considered solely a variable cost. However, there is a base amount of utilities that are fixed: every day the facility is open, there is a minimum amount of electricity, gas and water used. Therefore, utilities are generally segregated in an attempt to quantify the amount that is fixed and the amount that varies based on production.

- Other costs – Computers, software, employee benefits, travel and taxes are a few other expenses considered fixed. You'll notice that some of these costs are not "fixed" in our traditional understanding of the concept;

most of these items are somewhat discretionary in nature. While they may be discretionary, they do not fit the definition of direct costs either. If the operation is running efficiently, these costs are considered essential, but not direct, and therefore are a fixed cost of running the business.

It is important to note that this is not an exact science. All costs are fixed in the short-term and all costs are variable in the long-term. In other words, if the plant burned down tomorrow, you would have direct costs to pay, even though there are no sales and no production, and if sales and production doubled over the course of the year, you would need larger facilities and more support personnel. It is impossible and inefficient (remember cost/benefit?) to calculate to the penny which costs should be allocated to direct costs, and which are truly fixed. These are estimated, using your best judgement to help you understand the operation in a more meaningful way.

Cost of Goods Sold (Cost of Sales)

The variable, or direct costs each period are added together and divided up amongst the product manufactured to arrive at the true cost of the product produced. The product is either sold and shipped immediately or placed in inventory to be sold at a later date. When the product is sold, the cost of production is recognized in the income statement (profit and loss) as the cost of goods sold.

Example:

A widget factory produces 2 products in a 24-hour period: product A and product B. Product A takes twice as much time to manufacture, and it is sold 1.5 times as much as Product B. Raw materials are $3 for A and $5 per unit of B. Packaging materials are $0.80 and $1.00 respectively.

Product A		Product B	
Hours to manufacture	2	Hours to manufacture	1
# Manufactured	500	# Manufactured	1,000
Raw Materials	$1,500	Raw Materials	$5,000
Labor	$10,000	Labor	$5,000
Packaging Materials	$320	Packaging Materials	$1,000
Total Direct Costs	$11,820	Total Direct Costs	$11,000

Overhead is applied as a percentage of manufacturing time:

Overhead	
Supervisory Salaries	$2,000
Electricity	$1,000
Total	$3,000

Product A		Product B	
Total Direct Costs	$11,820	Total Direct Costs	$11,000
Overhead Applied	$2,000	Overhead Applied	$1,000
Total Cost	$13,820	Total Cost	$12,000

If the units are sold immediately, the cost of sales is the same as the total costs ($25,820). If the units are placed in inventory, the inventory value increases by $25,820. The direct costs are applied when the product moves from production to inventory.

For the sake of simplicity, let's assume that all items are sold immediately. In this case, the Cost of Goods Sold (cost of sales) is equal to the total direct costs plus the overhead applied.

	Product A		Product B	
Selling price per Unit	$30.00	Selling price per Unit	$20.00
Cost per Unit	$27.64	Cost per Unit	$12.00
Margin	$2.36	Margin	$8.00

Margin

The margin is the difference between the selling price and the cost to produce. Margin can be expressed on a per item basis, or as gross margin on the Income Statement.

Continuing the example above, assume that the selling price for Product A is $30 and the selling price for Product B is $20.

In this example, the margin of Product B is more than three times the margin of product A. Knowing this information will give management some food for thought: Is Product A priced appropriately? Can the cost per unit of A be reduced? What is the demand for Product A, versus Product B? Should we drop Product A altogether and focus production exclusively on B?

Taking our example further, reveals a total activity (in dollars):

Sales	$35,000
Cost of Goods Sold	$25,820
Gross Margin	$9,180

Margin is often expressed as a percentage of sales: gross margin / revenues. In this case the gross margin percentage is 9.18/35, or 26.23%.

Margin is a huge component in the profitability of manufacturing, retailing and wholesaling businesses and will be discussed in more detail later in the book.

Net Income

Net Income (profit) is the difference between gross margin and fixed costs.

Putting it All Together

Profitability is broken down into two major components: margin and fixed costs. If a company is not profitable, then the answer is found in one of these two components (or often, both).

Where to start?

Breakeven

Breakeven is the sales amount required in any given period that will yield neither profit nor loss. Knowing your breakeven point is a very important starting point in the analysis of your financials, especially with those companies that are losing money, or wavering each month between losing and making money.

In the example below, breakeven for a company with a 47% margin and $47 thousand in fixed costs is $100 thousand in sales:

SAMPLE Breakeven	
Sales	100,000
COGS	53,000
Margin	47,000
Fixed	47,000
Net Income	-

In this example, the company will lose money if they sell less than $100 thousand in any given period. It takes $100 thousand of sales dollars to cover the associated margins and fixed costs dollars that the company will incur for the period.

The formula for Breakeven is: Fixed Cost / Profit Margin (%)

Knowing the formula, helps you begin to see ways you might concentrate efforts in order to become more profitable. Your efforts should always be directed towards lowering the breakeven sales number. Why? Because the lower the breakeven number, the less sales that must be made in order to see profitability.

Here is what I mean:

In the same example, if fixed costs were lowered by 5%, to $44,650, then breakeven is calculated:

$44,650 / .47 = $95,000

In the same example, if the margin were increased by 5%, to 49.35%, then breakeven is calculated:

$47,000 / .4935 = $95,238

By reducing fixed costs by 5%, breakeven is lowered by $5,000. By increasing the margin by 5%, breakeven is lowered by only $4,761. From this, we can conclude that lowering fixed costs is more effective than increasing margins when attempting to lower our breakeven. A combination of the two, however, will yield even more effective results:

$44,650 / .4935 = $90,476

What does this mean for profits?

For every $1 in sales beyond the breakeven point, the company will make a profit equal to the gross margin percentage. In other words, once fixed costs are covered, every dollar sold will yield a profit equal to the gross margin percentage. If our company still sells $100,000, but the breakeven is now $90,476, it should expect to see profits of $4,700.

Sales	$100,000
Breakeven	$90,476
Difference	9,524
Margin %	49.35%
Profits	$4,700

Challenge: Calculate your company's current breakeven sales point. What would be a reasonable goal for reducing it?

Fixed Costs

Fixed costs, as you will recall, are the costs that do not tend to vary much from period to period, based on production. "Fixed", however, is a bit of a misnomer, because there is almost always a lot of discretionary spending found in fixed costs. You will also recall that lowering fixed costs has the most dramatic effect on your breakeven sales point, and that the key to increasing profitability, is to lower the breakeven point.

The best way to evaluate your fixed costs is to take each on an independent basis and justify it using some cost/benefit analysis that we discussed earlier. Be brutal in your thinking – even if you aren't ready to make decisions to cut, you should make yourself very aware of the consequences of each expense.

- Facility Rent – This is one of the most "fixed" of all fixed costs. But remember that all costs are variable in the long term. Take a look at the space you have now. Does it meet your needs? Is there more space than you need? Are you in a higher rent district than is warranted? Consider the following example:

A company currently has 30,000 sq feet of space on a lease of $1 per foot per month. It only needs about 22,000 sq feet of space. The owner finds a suitable piece of property that is 25,000 sq feet that leases at $1.10 per foot per month. Moving costs are estimated to be $20,000.

	Current Property	**Potential Property**
Monthly Rent	30,000	27,500
Annual Costs	360,000	330,000
Moving Costs	-	20,000
Total 1st Year Costs	360,000	350,000

In this example, the company would save $10 thousand in its first year by moving and $30 thousand each additional year.

Does this mean that the company should move immediately? Maybe, but not necessarily. There are certainly other factors to consider, such as accessibility to the target market. Rather than moving, there may be other opportunities take advantage of the additional space, such as subletting, or adding product lines. The point is to mathematically justify the use of space in a way that makes sense to the organization.

Salaries – Each employee should be justified in the same manner as other fixed costs. However, people are not your assets, and their contributions are much more complex to calculate than rent costs. As noted above, knowing your costs is the first step in addressing challenges. You may find that you have excess costs in salaried compensation, but terminating employees based solely on their mathematically calculated contribution would be a mistake. Creative thinking is often the key to managing employee costs.

- Management and span of control – Management salaries are usually the highest salary costs and often difficult to quantify. Since management only indirectly contributes to sales and income, it is inherently difficult to calculate their contributions on a cost/benefit basis. However, management salaries can be evaluated against other factors, such as operating results of the manager's department, performance against financial goals, salary comparisons to similar companies or against prior year results or budgets.
- Sales staff – Sales staff is compensated in a variety of ways, including a commission-only basis, a salaried basis, or some combination of the two. Their contributions are easily calculated: (Sales – Cost of Compensation) / Sales.)

In the following example, Salesperson A is compensated with 10% commission on sales,

Salesperson B is compensated with a flat salary of $120,000 and Salesperson C is compensated with a salary of $60,000 plus a commission of 5%. Sales for each is assumed to be $1.2 million. Payroll tax is calculated at 8% and benefits are assumed to be $20 thousand.

	Salesperson A	Salesperson B	Salesperson C
Salary	-	120,000	60,000
Commission	120,000	-	60,000
Taxes & Benefits	29,600	29,600	29,600
Total Costs	149,600	149,600	149,600
Sales	1,200,000	1,200,000	1,200,000
Contribution %	87.5%	87.5%	87.5%
Contribution $	1,050,400	1,050,400	1,050,400

As you can see from this example, the way the salesperson is paid, makes no difference in the amount he or she costs, as long as *sales remain constant*. It is widely held, however, that sales staff who work on commission only, or some combination, will hustle more and sell more. Let's say we buy into this assumption and recalculate, assuming that our commissioned based staffer (A) will sell 10% more, (B) will remain constant and (C) will sell 5% more. How does this change our calculations?

	Salesperson A	Salesperson B	Salesperson C
Salary	-	120,000	60,000
Commission	132,000	-	63,000
Taxes & Benefits	30,560	29,600	29,840
Total Costs	162,560	149,600	152,840
Sales	1,320,000	1,200,000	1,260,000
Contribution %	87.7%	87.5%	87.9%
Contribution $	1,157,440	1,050,400	1,107,160

If our assumption is true, salesperson A will contribute over $50 thousand more to our bottom line than salesperson C and more than $100 thousand more than Salesperson B. The caveat being, that our assumption must be true.

There are those that believe that Salesperson A will be under tremendous stress: if he/she doesn't sell anything, the family doesn't eat. This salesperson may look for work elsewhere. Salesperson B is under no stress: he/she gets paid regardless. Salesperson C may be under the optimal amount of stress to perform his/her best for the employer: the necessities of life are taken care of, but the extra income is well within reach. For this reason, it is incredibly important that you take the time to evaluate your assumptions to arrive at the most productive solution for your company.

As far as breakeven analysis is concerned, we have already established that reducing fixed costs has a greater impact than reducing variable costs. If your commissioned-only salesperson does not perform, your cost is greatly reduced. If your salaried salesperson does not perform, you are still stuck with a large fixed burden.

Let's assume now that you have 3 salespeople and pay each $60 thousand salary plus 5% commission per dollar sold. How much does each have to sell, in order for you to break even (assuming a margin of 40% and additional fixed costs of $1.2 million?)

As you will recall, the formula for Breakeven is: Fixed Cost / Profit Margin (%)

Total fixed costs for each sales rep is $460 thousand ($1.2 million divided by 3 reps plus his/her $60 thousand salary). The breakeven cost for each sales rep is calculated as $460,000/40% = $1,150,000.

This means that any sales rep who sales are less than $1,150,000 is actually **costing** the company money. Each dollar sold above that threshold will make the company 40 cents.

Challenge: Calculate the breakeven sales amount for each of your sales reps. In what ways would changing your compensation structure affect this amount?

- o Admin staff – Admin staff is an extremely important cog in the wheel of business: customer service reps, human resource personnel and, of course, accountants perform vital services, but, like management, it can be difficult to quantify their contributions. A good customer service rep may soothe angry customers and may save many from walking away, but there is really no way to measure that contribution with any certainty. A good human resources manager understands the complexities of employment law and thus, saves the company from needless lawsuits, but this is only apparent in the absence of a good human resources manager. A good staff accountant will keep excellent records and save the company from a multitude of fines, but that cannot be measured either. Here are a few ideas for "rethinking" admin costs:

- Job sharing – 2 part-time employees doing the work of 1 full time employee equates to lower benefit costs and flexible workplace.
- Sometimes a bookkeeping firm or CPA firm can do the work cheaper and better than your full-time accountant. Human resource and customer service jobs can also be outsourced.
- Think globally. I know many business owners who utilize workers from overseas for admin work.
- Insurance, Utilities, Employee benefits, monthly subscriptions, etc. – These fixed costs are only fixed in the short run. Insurance and benefits

can be re-evaluated every year and savings can always be found. Utilities can be monitored and can often be controlled with minimal investments in some low tech solutions, such as changing lightbulbs or using motion detectors. As of this writing, there are tax incentives on the purchase of larger equipment that can help bring about energy savings. Monthly subscriptions for software, internet, phone, etc. are often very small on an individual basis, but in the aggregate may provide fixed cost savings by shopping around or eliminating services that have duplicate features.

- Meals -This category is generally not one of the largest costs, but I believe that it's a very important one to address, because I think it goes to the very heart of what holds a lot of small businesses back: the fear of making too much money, because the tax bill will be crippling. Let me get this part out of the way first: there are a lot of rules about the deductibility of meals, but as a general rule, your daily breakfast and lunch are not legally deductible. The problem is that our tax law is anti-business. The tax laws encourage spending and encourage inefficiency. The more money a business makes, the more taxes it will pay. It's as if the government wants your business to fail.

In desperation to reduce tax bills, many small businesses have developed a mentality to 'spend more to save more' or to try to reclassify personal expenses to business expenses. This is all well and good (except for the legality, of course), but most of us do not approach our spending for the two in the same way. As business owners, we think about the bottom line (or at least we should), we think carefully about our spending options (or at least we should), we look at spending as an investment (you know what I'm thinking), but as personal individuals, as consumers, we think more about personal pleasure, we think about the wants and needs of our families, we compromise.

Most business owners, I think are careful with their finances. Many individuals are a bit more relaxed in their spending. If these two "spending personalities" are competing for dollars in your business, you may find that the waters get a bit muddy.

Legal and psychological issues aside, does 'spending more to save more' make economic sense? Let's look at how the meal deduction works.

Let's assume that a business owner stops for Starbucks every morning and Subway every lunchtime and charges those against the business account in an effort to reduce the tax liability. Let's further assume for the sake of argument, that all these meals are deductible (and clearly, they are not). If you stopped at Starbucks every morning and ordered a large (Venti, for you aficionados) coffee and breakfast sandwich, and

Subway every day for lunch and ordered a 6-inch combo with chips and a drink, you'd spend around $3,600 in "business meals". I'm using quotes facetiously, because, remember, these do NOT meet the IRS requirements of business meals. The IRS only allows deductibility of ½ of business meals, so the deduction is reduced by $1,800. Assuming a 20% overall effective tax rate, you would save a total of $360. Is that worth creating a potential IRS red flag? Compare that to my totally unscientific calculations found on the internet, and you'll see that you'd spend roughly $940 making the same meals at home each day. According to these calculations, this strategy will actually cost you around $2,400 each year:

	Take Out	Homemade
Total Cost	$3,628	$939
Tax break at effective tax rate of 20%	(363)	-
Total Cost	$3,265	$939

There may be many reasons for choosing to eat your meals out each day, but clearly, it is not an effective tax strategy to spend an extra $2,689, in order to save $363.

Margin

As noted above, the margin is one of the two factors that affect profitability. As you will remember, the margin is calculated as the total sales less the direct costs associated with those sales. Direct costs are sometimes used interchangeably with variable costs (costs that are not the same each month but vary with sales or production). The margin divided by the gross sales is called the contribution margin. The higher the contribution margin, the lower the breakeven point for sales and, theoretically, profits. Therefore, it is in a company's best interest to study its contribution margin and continually work towards raising it.

Let's look at the two factors affecting margin: sales and direct costs.

Sales

Total sales can be manipulated in one of two ways: either change the selling price or change the number of units sold.

- Selling price – There are many factors that affect the market's sensitivity towards price, including the commoditization/specialization of goods sold, lead time, return policies, supply and demand, customer service and on and on. All of these factors are important to consider before changing prices but are beyond the scope of this material. Here we will only discuss how price changes affect the margin and overall profitability of a company.

    Assume the following breakeven sample:

SAMPLE Breakeven	
Sales	100,000
COGS	53,000
Margin	47,000
Fixed	47,000
Net Income	-

In this example, the contribution margin is 47%. Let's assume that the company raises its sales price by 5%. Further assume that the market is not very price sensitive at this range. The new calculation looks like this:

Sales	105,000
COGS	53,000
Margin	52,000
Fixed	47,000
Net Income	5,000

The margin is now almost 50% ($52,000/$105,000) and profitability has risen by $5 thousand. Note that breakeven sales number is unchanged. It still requires the same *dollar* amount in sales to break even, but fewer *units* will be required to attain it.

Let's take the example a bit further and assume that in the first example each unit cost $10. The company sells 10,000 units and breaks even. In the second example, the company still sells 10,000 units, but at $10.50 each to make a $5 thousand profit. What if the market is somewhat sensitive to price? Let's assume that if the company raises prices 5%, that the sales volume will also decrease by 5%.

Sales	99,750
COGS	50,350
Margin	49,400
Fixed	47,000
Net Income	2,400

In this example, total sales volume is reduced (10,000 units drops to 9,500), COGS is reduced (95% of $53,000) and net income decreases as well ($5,000 versus $2,400). But because the margin is around 50%, sales volume must decrease at twice the rate of the selling price increase in order to hit breakeven again (9,000 units):

Sales	94,500
COGS	47,700
Margin	46,800
Fixed	47,000
Net Income	(200)

Thus, in our example, by raising our prices 5%, we can still reach breakeven (or very close), even if demand drops by 10%.

o Sales volume - If the market is very sensitive to price, increases in overall sales may only be achieved by increasing the volume sold. This is a much more difficult way to increase income, because changes in volume will not change the contribution margin. Total sales will go up, but the cost of sales will go up in the same percentage, thus resulting in a smaller profit based on the same amount of sales dollars:

Sales = (10,000*1.05= 10,500 *$10) COGS = ($105,000 * .47 contribution margin)

Sales	105,000
COGS	55,650
Margin	49,350
Fixed	47,000
Net Income	2,350

Therefore, we can conclude that an increase in selling price is the more efficient method for increasing revenues.

Direct Costs

Another way to increase the contribution margin and thereby lower the breakeven point, is by decreasing the costs directly attributable to the production and sale of the product. Direct costs have two components: direct labor, direct materials.

- Direct labor - Labor often composes the largest portion of the cost of sales, but it is also one of the most difficult to control. Labor equates to people, and there is no easy solution that works in all cases. Reducing the wage rate is difficult, and a rarely used tactic. Layoffs are much more common, but, in my opinion, often rash and short-sited. For every challenge, however, there is a solution. Remember, a change of only a few percentage points in the margin can mean a big difference in profitability. Sometimes, a little creativity is required.

- Overtime – Overtime rates are 1.5 to 2 times regular pay rates, so it is often in your best interest to limit their use. As we discussed in an earlier chapter, work should generally be assigned to the lowest paid, *capable* person. This is even more important when overtime is being paid. It is infinitely better to pay $22.50 per hour for a job, than $30.00 per hour ($15 straight time versus $20). Ask yourself if overtime is absolutely necessary. Almost all companies have a policy that overtime must be approved in advance by the supervisor, but how many supervisors do the math to see if the cost/benefit pans out for their employers?
- Outside contractors – Controlling the costs of outside contractors is generally much easier that controlling the cost of your own employee time. This is because the contractor will set the price beforehand and generally takes on the risk of

finishing on-time and under budget. In exchange, the outside contractor will usually demand a higher payment than you would pay an employee.

However, you must weigh this higher cost against the benefits of a reduction in payroll taxes. Additionally, outside contractors may be a good option if the work you offer is not steady or is seasonal. You won't have to pay for employee's time when there is little work to be done. There are intangible costs that should be considered, as well. You will not have as much control over the process or the timing of the project completion with outside contractors as you would with your own employees. After all, contractors are professionals who generally work on many projects for many different companies. One final note on outside contractors: federal and state law require business owners to evaluate personnel and classify according to many legal factors. **You may not choose to treat employees as contractors in order to save money on payroll taxes.** Some types of work are easily classified. You could hire a janitor in house or hire a janitorial service company to clean up. Others are less obvious. Hairdressers, for example, working in a salon may be classified as employees under certain circumstances and outside contractors, in others. Please be sure to evaluate state and federal law carefully when making this distinction.

When thinking of margins and breakeven analysis, we often think of large, complex organizations, such as manufacturers, but service businesses can also use this method to obtain extraordinary results. For an example, let's take a case study of a housekeeping business:

> Spic and Span Housecleaning is owned by two equal partners. They currently have 2 part-time employees who work a total of 160 hours per month. Total employee costs are $20 per hour and both Pat and Penny are taking salaries of $6,500 per month. They charge their clients $150 per hour for cleaning. They

have already calculated their break-even sales at $24,000 per month. They would love to hire a new manager because they are finding that between sales calls and administrative work, not to mention jumping in and helping clean houses occasionally, they are overwhelmed at the thought of bringing in new business.

Their Income Statement looks like this:

	Monthly Income
Sales	24,000
Cost of Labor	3,200
Supplies	1,200
Margin	19,600
Salaries	16,000
Rent	3,000
Other	3,600
Total Fixed	19,600
Net Income	0

Bringing in a new manager would definitely take some of the pressure off of Pat and Penny, but adding an extra $3,000 of fixed costs to their income statement would put them out of business in a hurry:

	Monthly Income
Sales	24,000
Cost of Labor	3,200
Supplies	1,200
Margin	19,600
Salaries	16,000
Rent	3,000
Other	3,600
Total Fixed	22,600
Net Loss	(3,000)

Arguably, having the manager would free up a bit of time for both Pat and Penny and they can presumably find more work. Sales would inevitably increase, but the break- even sales to cover this manager now looks like this:

	Monthly Income
Sales	27,675
Cost of Labor	3,690
Supplies	1,384
Margin	22,601
Salaries	16,000
Rent	3,000
Other	3,601
Total Fixed	22,601
Net Loss	0

This equates to about 24 hours per month of work. But who is to do the work? Add more hours to existing employees, does the manager assume some of the work? Does this even make sense? This tiny company now has 3 managers to oversee 2 part-time employees! Is there a way to leverage their fixed costs in such a way as to bring in more sales, using their existing employee structure?

A typical span of control for lower level management is 3-4. There should be a way this partnership can handle all the aspects of the business and still increase their profitability. In a perfect scenario, Pat and Penny should divide up their efforts to make sure that all responsibilities are met, and each has very specific duties. Whichever is the best salesperson should take on the sales role and run with it. The other should take over the admin and management duties and run with it. Neither should ever clean houses.

If Pat is the better salesperson, Pat should spend 8 hours every day pursuing sales. Penny would then concentrate all of her efforts on running the business and managing the employees. If each of their talents was leveraged in this way, they could add 2 full-time employees to their existing structure (320 more hours a week of work), before ever having to add that second manager. Now their Profit and Loss statement looks something like this:

	Monthly Income
Sales	72,000
Cost of Labor	9,600
Supplies	3,600
Margin	58,800
Salaries	13,000
Rent	3,000
Other	3,601
Total Fixed	19,601
Net Profit	39,199

If they can keep fixed costs at these levels over a period of time, and leverage them to their fullest potential, their profits will skyrocket.

When times get tough, many businesses look for ways to cut cost. How many times to do you hear companies talking about layoffs. There are many times when this is the correct strategy and it is always a good idea to keep your fixed costs as lean as possible. You should continually look at your fixed costs to determine which costs are contributing to your business in a positive way and which are just an added expense. However, lowering fixed costs will only get you so far.

In our example above, fixed costs were only $19k (and $13k of it was owners' salary). Realistically, there are only a few places where costs can be cut. Increasing profits is very difficult by cost-cutting alone. Leveraging assets and fixed costs to increase margins, and thereby profits, is mathematically the better course of action. There is literally no ceiling placed on the amount that your profits can increase!

Chapter 9
DEBT

The Good, the Bad, and the Ugly

Sooner or later, almost all business owners will run into cash flow problems. They may need to purchase some great piece of equipment that will surely revolutionize their operations, or they are offered a big bargain on inventory from a competitor's closing, or they just can't make payroll this month because their Accounts Receivable didn't come through as planned. For these types of situations, many owners will take out loans or use credit cards to cover the shortfall.

Before Jumping Into Debt, There Are Some Important Points To Consider

What is the money being used for? - Most owners believe loans are there to pay for purchases that they need or think they need, when there is no company money on hand. This is not how debt should be used.

Recall from an earlier chapter that there are two basic types of purchases: assets and expenses. Assets are purchases that will benefit future periods and expenses are purchases that are used up immediately. Examples of assets are factory equipment, real estate, inventory, warehouse racks, office furniture, computers and printers. Expenses are utilities, rent, payroll. Although the people themselves should benefit the company in the future, generally by the time they are paid, their company has already reaped the benefits of their labor.

Assets, by definition, are used in the production of income (or the reduction of a cost). New machinery may be more efficient than the old and thus increase production in a manufacturing plant; a new forklift may decrease the wear and tear on employees' backs and reduce workers' comp costs; purchasing an office building will decrease rental expenses and the property itself will likely appreciate in the future; inventory can be sold at a later date for profit.

Which Seems Worthier Of A Loan?

Expenses, on the other hand, are costs that benefit the company immediately. Although electricity is a necessity, paying June's bill will not increase July's productivity; wages spent today helps to ensure that some of your workers will stick around for another week, but you will surely have to pay them again at the end of next week; donuts purchased for the office, once passed the lips will be forever on the hips, but will not benefit the future of the company in any tangible way.

It should be obvious that going into debt to purchase assets is far more reasonable than going into debt to cover current expenses. Why? Presumably, the assets *themselves* will help create the income to pay off the debt. If you go into debt to pay past expenses, what is the plan to make additional income to pay off the loan? It becomes a vicious cycle: current revenues must be used to pay past debts, so therefore, more debt must be attained to cover current expenses. As the months pass, not only does the debt increase, but the interest expense also increases, making it increasingly more difficult to dig out of the hole.

Some will argue that paying off credit card balances each month is a legitimate strategy. It is, in effect, an interest-free 30- day loan. Others will say that they benefit from cash back on credit card purchases or use them exclusively for the points and benefits. These statements are all very reasonable and work for some business owners. However, it's been my experience that most business owners rely way too heavily on credit cards and do not maintain high enough cash balances to even-out the ebb and flow of the business cycle.

Let's take a look at an example:

Dr. D is a dermatologist whose business is built around a fat serum injection to eliminate wrinkles. One month, he learns that the serum has been linked to cancer and his sales declines that month 10%. He has some cash in an emergency fund.

Scenario 1: Dr. D is worried about the future of the serum, so he thinks he'd better hold onto his cash and takes out a working capital loan of $20,000 at 6% annual interest for 2 years. Monthly payments are $886.

Scenario 2: Dr. D is worried about the future of the serum. He does some research and finds out that he can purchase a used laser for $20,000 that will erase wrinkles without any side effects. He believes that if he really works hard, the laser treatments can become 15% of his business. He takes out a business loan at 6% annual interest for 2 years. Monthly payments are $886.

Assume that the fat serum business does not recover, and revenues hold flat at 90%. Assume also a 40% margin for both products.

Dr. D Average Income		
	Monthly	Annual
Sales	100,000	1,200,000
Cost of Sales	60,000	720,000
Gross Margin	40,000	480,000

Dr. D Estimated Year 1		
	Working Capital Loan	Equipment Loan
Sales		
Fat Serum	1,080,000	1,080,000
Laser	-	162,000
Cost of Sales		
Fat Serum	648,000	648,000
Laser	-	97,200
Gross Margin	432,000	496,800
Cash Flow		
Revenue	(48,000)	16,800
Cash from WC Loan	20,000	-
Debt Payment	(10,637)	(10,637)
Change in Cash flow	(38,637)	6,163

As you can see, the working capital loan does nothing to help Dr. D stay in business, other than to inject a bit of cash in the short-term. Not shown in the example, is another problem: If Dr. D only has a small amount of cash saved, he may have a difficult time making the payments on the loan. He may have to take out a second loan to further finance the expenses of the operation, or resort to credit card debt. Either way, his cash flow problem will only increase.

The equipment loan, on the other hand, finances an asset that can be used to produce income in the future. Even if Dr. D's estimates are way off, he is still better off with the equipment loan. His sales estimate may be too high, but he will surely sell some product. His margin estimate may also be too high, but there will surely be some return. Even If the equipment fails all together, he has an asset that presumably has some value in the marketplace that he can sell.

Chapter 10
INTERNAL CONTROLS

Keeping What's Yours

Now that you've worked hard and earned all this extra money, wouldn't you like an insurance policy that protects you from employee theft? If you're like most small business owners I know, you will answer "no" to this question. Why? The answer is obvious: you only hire the best, most trustworthy employees, so no one would ever steal from you, right? And yet, employee theft is a huge problem. According to Hiscox Insurance, small and midsize businesses were hit with 68 percent of the employee theft losses filed in 2016. Their median loss that year was $289,864.

And who are these people that are victims of employee theft? Are they the ones that hire all the "bad" people? When Bob, the owner of a small business learns that Nancy, his office manager has paid her mortgage through his bank account 4 times in the last year, does he say to himself, "Darn it! It serves me right for having a policy of only hiring bad people. If only I'd listened to all my friends and looked for trustworthy people, I wouldn't be in this mess today."

Of course not! Up until the moment that Bob's tax guy congratulated him on his "new home" and asked for the closing docs, Nancy was one of the 'good and trustworthy' employees who would never steal from him. They were like family: when Nancy got married last year, Bob hosted the reception in his back yard. When Bob had hernia surgery in August, Nancy took a casserole to his wife for dinner. No one with that type of relationship would ever steal from him…right?

Here is the truth: good people sometimes make poor choices.

Don't take my word for it, there is some science that backs this up. It's called the Fraud Triangle. According to this theory, first put forth by Donald Cressey, after interviewing 200 embezzlers, fraud is most likely to occur when the following three conditions are present: Pressure, opportunity and Justification.

Let's talk about each one in turn.

Pressure

Remember Nancy's wedding reception? Everyone had a great time, but Stuart, the groom, was having the time of his life. He and Jack Daniels were clearly best buds and he danced with all the girls, sang with the band and told stories into the night. At about 2:00 am, the exhausted bride poured her stinking drunk husband into the passenger side of her car, apologized to Bob for Stuart's rowdiness and drove off towards happily ever after.

Six months later, Stuart was arrested for driving under the influence. He was thrown in jail, and his driver's license was revoked. Stuart was employed as a delivery driver, so when he lost his license, he also lost his job.

The "good and trustworthy" Nancy, who was barely getting by before marriage, now finds herself with the same mound of bills she always had, plus some crippling legal fees heaped on top, not to mention another mouth to feed, and no relief to be found in the immediate future.

What's a girl to do?

Opportunity

Bob likes to hire good people because he's a busy guy and there are things he's not very good at…things that he doesn't like to do that still need to get done. He's listened to the advice in this book and in others and knows that delegating is the way to go.

Bob hates finances. He hates billing, writing checks and reconciling bank statements. In fact, he hates even thinking about these things. He was excited when he found Nancy ten years ago, because she was so competent. She likes doing all those things, and since he hired her, his problems of bounced checks and unpaid bills have vanished.

He knows he should keep an eye on his own finances, but he trusts Nancy. She's never given him any reason not to (although, how would he know, really), so five years ago, when she'd suggested that he add her as a signer to the account, he'd thought it was a great idea. That way, he reasoned, there was no interruption in business when he was out of town. Two years ago, she'd suggested that they receive the bank statements online. She'd reasoned that she wouldn't have to wait for the statements to come in the mail. Bob had thought it was a great idea, too. He still had access to the statements, of course, but he can't remember the last time he'd looked at one.

Justification

'Bob's business is booming', thinks Nancy. 'He has so much money coming in, he doesn't know what to do with it. And he makes such frivolous choices', she thinks. 'He wastes so much money on going out to eat every day; he goes to all those concerts; he buys tickets to football games, baseball games, soccer games; he lives like a king! And his wife', she thinks, 'his wife has to have the best of everything. Who is she to drive around in a new car every year? And those family trips! Lord, they must spend $20 thousand a year, just on trips. And don't get me started on those "children" of his...full grown and should be on their own...'

'You know, I really do a lot around here', she continues. 'When I started, I really thought he was paying me well, but I think, considering everything I do for him, I should be making more. It's like I'm responsible for everything around here! In fact, if I really think about it, Bob definitely wouldn't be where he is today without me. When was the last time I got a raise?'

'Bob really would feel bad for me if he knew my situation. I'm sure, if he knew what was going on, he would loan me as much money as I needed. I hate to bother him with it, though. He's so busy and I don't want to embarrass Stuart. I don't want Bob to think poorly of him and I know he's learned his lesson this time.'

'Stuart will be getting a job just as soon as he gets back on his feet -probably even by next month. I just need enough to pay the mortgage this month, and then next month Stuart will have a job and we can pay it back. I could write a check for the mortgage this month out of Bob's account - he never pays any attention anyway and pay it back next month.'

'No one ever has to know'.

In our example with Bob and Nancy, the three legs: pressure, opportunity and justification, come together to form the perfect fraud triangle.

Take away one leg, though, and you no longer have a triangle: the likelihood of fraud is drastically reduced. Which leg is under the employers' control?

Every human being on earth has pressures: there are always mortgage payments to be made, cars to be repaired, kids to bail out of jail, bookies to be paid. In a nutshell, life happens. As an employer, how much control do you have over your employees' lives? How much do you even know about you employees? You may think you are one happy family, but don't kid yourself. Your employees have lives that have nothing to do with you or your company. You have little to no control over their needs and problems.

Justification is simply a lie you tell yourself, and every human being on earth does it. If you can justify that your daily Starbucks run is a business expense and Jack the Ripper could justify that he was cleansing London of prostitutes, then surely it isn't too large of a leap to imagine that Nancy justifies paying her mortgage right out of your bank account. It doesn't matter how much you pay your employees, how great of a relationship you have with them or how carefully you chose them in the first place, you have no defense against another human being's capacity to lie to himself. Deep, deep down inside, I think we all know when we are justifying our own poor behavior – that is why we rarely talk about it. We know if we repeat our justifications out loud to another human being, we might get called upon it.

That is why you have no defense against Nancy's justification for stealing from you: she will keep her justification secret from you and probably everyone else, so you have no opportunity to address her concerns directly.

By process of elimination, we know that opportunity is the only leg of the triangle where the employer may exercise control. The employer has control over who signs checks, who reconciles the bank account, who touches the cash, who invoices the customer, who issues credit memos and who writes off the bad debt.

We call these internal controls: policies and procedures that make sure that everything that should get billed, does get billed, everything that should get paid, does get paid and nothing that shouldn't, doesn't.

Accountants love good internal controls, but everybody else hates them. Why is this? I have a few theories. First of all, internal controls are boring and tedious and made up by a bunch of bean counters to make life miserable for everyone else. (Sorry if that comes off a little snarky. As a former auditor, I've witnessed a lot of negative reactions to this topic.) In defense of bean counters everywhere, I'd like to say that internal controls are developed for YOUR benefit, to help you run efficiently and reduce the opportunity for theft or fraud.

Secondly, I believe that everyone hates internal controls because they are uncomfortable and embarrassing. After all, telling Nancy that you are now requiring a second signature on all checks is tantamount to telling Nancy that she is probably a thief and you know all about her no-good husband. This is a feeble excuse, of course. As a business owner, you know there are many decisions you must make that are difficult.

Finally, everyone hates internal controls because they really don't understand them. If you routinely perform a procedure, but don't know why, you probably aren't doing it right and you won't get the results that the procedure was designed for anyway. I honestly believe that if business owners understood just a few controls better, implemented them and followed up, there would be much, much less theft in the workplace.

With that in mind, I'd like to introduce a few concepts:

Separation of Duties- In accounting, there are three distinct functions that, if separated, will greatly reduce theft. The functions are custody, authorization and record keeping.

Custody is the function of keeping assets safe. The person that has the key to the petty cash drawer has custody of the petty cash. The person who has keys to the office has custody of the assets inside.

Authorization is the function of having the authority to put those assets in use or make obligations on the company's behalf. An authorizer signs purchase orders and contracts, uses credit cards or signs checks.

Record keeping is the function of entering transactions into the company's financial system. Record keeper's do the bookkeeping, reconcile bank statements and enter payroll transactions.

Let's go back to the example with Bob and Nancy. In the beginning, Bob performed most of the accounting functions himself. Over time, though, he gave up many of the functions to Nancy because she was much better at the various tasks and because he didn't like to do them. At the time Nancy needed the money, she had control over all three functions:

- Nancy has custody over the bank account. She shares access to the bank statement with Bob, but he has totally abdicated this responsibility to her.
- Nancy has authorization over making purchases. She is now a signer on the bank account (for emergencies only), but over time, Bob has abdicated this responsibility, as well. She now signs all the checks. (By the way, when auditing, I always hear that the bookkeeper has signing authority for "emergencies only" and rarely uses the privilege. In fact, it doesn't matter whether or not the bookkeeper uses the privilege or not, the mere fact that she has been given signing authority completely negates the benefit of

segregating the duties. If she has the *option* of signing a check and that check will likely never be viewed or questioned by anyone else, there is opportunity for fraud.)

- o Nancy has record keeping duties. She enters the transaction into the financial system and later reconciles the bank account.

Nancy can easily steal money, and it is unlikely that she will ever get caught, because no one else is involved. If just one of these functions was given to another person, the likelihood is greatly diminished. It is much less likely that a person will steal or commit fraud if they know that someone is reviewing their work, or if they must convince another person to look the other way or co-conspire with them.

If Bob still got the bank statement and reviewed it before passing it on to Nancy, he would likely see the mortgage payments being made and ask questions of either Nancy or the bank. If Bob had not made Nancy a signer on the account, he surely would have noticed that he was paying Nancy's mortgage when he signed the checks. If Bob reconciled the bank account, it is likely that he would have noticed the payments.

It is perfectly acceptable for Bob to delegate these tasks. He can separate the duties between Nancy and another employee. However, there is a difference between delegating responsibilities and abdicating them. Delegating responsibilities means that Bob is having his employees work on these tasks on his behalf; abdicating means that he is giving up the responsibility for them. This is a distinction that must be understood. Every business owner or manager should be involved in his own finances. He should be able to read a financial statement. He should review his own bank statements and reconciliations, at least on occasion.

Accounting System Access Control- Give your employees access to your accounting system on a 'need to know' basis.

Make sure that everyone has a unique password and that passwords are not shared or written on a sticky note and stuck to the computer screen. (Again, you would be surprised what you see as an auditor). This is another layer of control that reduces the opportunity for theft or fraud.

Some examples:

- Allow Human Resources access to adding employees and pay rates, but not hours worked or writing checks. Payroll has access to hours worked and writing checks, but not to adding employees or pay rates. This allows the payroll department to pay according to hours worked, but does not allow them to change their own pay rates (or anyone else's) or enter a paycheck for their next door neighbor, girlfriend or mother. Meanwhile, you allow human resources to set up employees, but not allowing them to write checks.
- Allow one employee access to billing customers and another to receiving payments. This a deterrent from changing invoices and pocketing the extra money.

- Separate passwords create an audit trail. If everyone shares a password, it is impossible to tell which user is responsible for suspicious activity.

Physical Audit of Assets – If you've recorded inventory and capital assets correctly, your accounting system can supply a list of items that should be under company control. Periodic counts of these items should be taken and compared against records. Large variances should be investigated.

Standardize Documentation – Using pre-numbered, standardized documentation, such as purchase orders, check requests and expense reports creates consistency and reduces confusion, which in turn, reduces the occurrences of fraud, theft and mistakes. Accounting systems can be created to recognize duplicate numbers or give warnings for lack of correct documentation.

For example, the accounting system will not allow a payment for an invoice unless there is a valid purchase order and receiving document (bill of lading) and the invoice matches the purchase price on the purchase order and the number of goods received. This may be an elaborate system for a small company, but even small companies can benefit by using some forms of standardized documentation such as signed check requests or expense reports with proper source documentation attached. The more disciplined the approach to accounting, the more difficult it is for a justifying employee to take advantage of the chaos.

Periodic Review of Financial Information – In this book, we have preached about understanding and using your financial information to make better decisions. If you have the attitude that the only use for your financial statements is to file a tax return, you probably haven't made it this far in the book. However, understanding your financial statements is also a great internal control. If you recognize that relationships between certain numbers are out of the ordinary, or that balances are not in line with your expectations, you are much better prepared to recognize fraud when you see it. Budgets are also great at fraud detection. A well thought out budget not only guides you in your decision-making throughout the business cycle, it can also highlight variances to expectations that should be investigated.

Reconciliation – Periodic reconciliation of your records to outside sources is a great way to catch errors and deter and detect fraud. That being said, I believe there is a huge misunderstanding today of what exactly is reconciliation.

In the old days, when you purchased something, you paid with either cash or a check. When you sold something, you were paid with either cash or check. About a week after the end of each month, the bank sent out what we called a bank statement in the mail (holy cow! The mail!) that captured all those transactions. The crazy thing was, we didn't know what our bank balance was until we received the statement. In order to know how much money there was in the bank, we would have to record each time we spent money or received money in a ledger and keep a running total of the balance. When we received the statement, we would compare our running total to the amount on the bank statement and then explain any differences. This is what we called 'reconciling'. If there were any transactions that were suspect, they were caught through this manual process.

In an effort to speed things up and make data entry more efficient, accounting software has taken all the manual effort out of recording transactions. We now have bank feeds and automatic 'reconciliations.' However, if the bank provides the feed and the statement, are we not just reconciling the bank records to the bank records? While this gives us values and efficiencies, it does not offer any real internal control.

A person can (and almost always does) 'reconcile' bank accounts without truly looking at any of the transactions. The reconciliation feature produces a report that shows the difference between what is in the accounting system and what is on the bank balance. Those variances are marked as 'uncleared' items. In the traditional sense, 'uncleared' items meant transactions that had not yet cleared the bank, such as checks that had not been cashed, or occasionally, a deposit in transit. Today, though, 'uncleared' often means 'error'. In today's world, deposits are often cleared on the same day. Credit, eft, debit cards are real time or perhaps with a day or two lag-time. Yet, almost every time I view a new client's books, I will find 'uncleared' transactions that are months or even years old. Obviously, these are errors that have yet to be addressed. But if you ask the owner, she will tell you that the books are reconciled and point to the report you are holding in your hand. This tells me that there is a huge gap in understanding the reconciliation function as it has evolved today.

In order to have a decent internal control, you must truly understand the transactions in your bank account and work to understand and reduce the errors. I once saw a bookkeeper steal in the following way:

> Ken is responsible for writing checks and reconciling the bank account. His boss, Dr. Barbie, when not in surgery, is flying off in her private plane to the dreamhouse and pays little attention to the finances. She just wants to see the bottom line. Ken has noticed that the bookkeeper, Skipper makes a lot of mistakes. Over the last year, about $60,000 of uncashed checks have accumulated in the 'uncleared' section of the reconciliation. Ken knows that these are not true uncashed checks. He writes a check for himself for $60k and voids the uncashed checks in the accounting records, in effect changing the bank balance by $0. Barbie never notices, Ken has his own Corvette now and Skipper will continue to inadvertently supply him

with the extra cash he'll need for living the life that Barbie stole from him...(remember justification?)

Approval Limits – Each person that has approval authority should have limits on that authority (e,g, a supervisor may have a purchasing limit of $500, a manager $1,000 and the owner is unlimited). This works to minimize the amount an individual could steal to the amount of his authority level. Of course, there must be a system in place to enforce the limits. Credit cards are easy to limit this way. The card issuer can limit the amount per transaction and per month for employees based on the criteria established by company management. While the likelihood of large-scale fraud is diminished, approval limits will not work to deter or detect smaller occurrences.

All of the aforementioned are great internal controls designed to keep your assets safe and thus explain the theory behind internal controls. If you are looking for a quick and dirty list, I've compiled my Top 10 internal controls below:

Top 10 Internal Controls

1. Pay attention to office gossip (but never gossip yourself. I hate it and it's totally unprofessional). If it's rumored that one of your accounting employees may have financial troubles, you may want to pay attention.
2. Two people should always count cash, then seal it up and deposit immediately.
3. Consider hiring an accounting firm to review or audit your books.
4. Owners and management should study the financial reports, ask questions, view copies of checks written, inquire about unusual items.
5. Create an annual operating budget and separate budgets for each department. Compare actual results against budgeted amounts and prior years.
6. Require 2 signatures for check-writing.

7. **Standardize your procedures using preformatted forms, standardized email addresses, etc. Be organized.**
8. **Limit the number of cash handlers. Cash handlers should not be the same people who record the transactions or reconcile the bank account.**
9. **Reconcile the bank account every month. Inquire about anything odd.**
10. **Pay attention, communicate, follow up, be a leader!**

Remember, Internal controls, when designed and implemented well, can reduce the likelihood of errors, theft and fraud.

Chapter 11
COMMON ERRORS

Would you Jump Off a Cliff Just Because Everyone Else was Doing It?

While everyone's situation is unique, I've noticed over the years that there are a handful of common traps that business tend to fall into. For that reason, we've decided to dedicate a chapter to the discussion of these.

Do-it-Yourselfers – I am a big do-it-yourselfer. I watch a tv show on house flipping and decide that I'm an interior decorator. I have been known to paint my own bedrooms, sew my own curtains, refurbish furniture pieces and once or twice, even lay my own tile. I get personal satisfaction out of doing things myself. I like the creative process; I like pushing my boundaries and besides, it's my house and if it doesn't work out, I can always hire someone to fix it.

I have my boundaries, of course. I might unclog a drain, but I would never re-pipe a bathroom (I don't really even know what that means!) I might make a tablecloth, but certainly never a table. I know my limits.

Doing it myself in my business, however, is another matter. I want my business to be a money-making machine. I want it to be streamlined and efficient. I may write books on the side, but I don't write the copy on my own web site: I save my creative urges for my house. I want my time at work to be laser focused on what I do best and what will bring me the most return. Everything else can be delegated to employees or hired out.

We've discussed, at length, that all jobs in your business should be filled by the lowest paid, most capable person. Where does the accounting/bookkeeping function fall into this equation? It should be approached using the same type of logic that we've taught in other areas. Accounting is a skill and a discipline. QuickBooks has tried to teach us that their software is so intuitive that everyone is an accountant, but that just isn't so. I'm all for lowest paid, but if your guy isn't capable, you're getting nothing for your money.

But if you're no accountant, how can you judge the accounting skills of others? Luckily for you, we anticipated this question, and developed a quick test for the purpose of rating others. Email me today for a copy. You may use this test when hiring a new bookkeeper or evaluating your current accountant. If your guy doesn't pass, that means he's not competent enough to handle your books.

Thinking Cash Accounting Is Good Enough - Although cash is king and it is all anyone really cares about, accrual accounting is far, far superior when it comes to analyzing finances. This sounds counterintuitive, but accrual accounting, once you understand it, makes much more sense. One of the great tenants of accrual accounting is that it matches expenses incurred to revenues in the period in which they were earned. If raw materials were purchased in January, product was manufactured in February, shipped and billed in March and payment was received in April, you will get wildly different results using cash and accrual methods. If following the cash method, January and February will report losses and May will produce a profit. You will "feel like" your business was a loser for the first three months and wonder what you are doing wrong, only to find that in April, the only month where you actually contributed nothing to the process, you are suddenly successful! Overall, was the product run profitable? It is impossible to tell without converting the processes back into the accrual framework.

Payroll Amounts Are Recorded Incorrectly – Payroll and payroll taxes are probably the two most misunderstood elements of an average small business owners' income statement. Most bookkeepers will record the net paycheck as wages and the amount paid to the IRS and other taxing authorities as taxes. This is INCORRECT. In the end, the total expense may (or may not) be recorded correctly, but how does that help a business owner who wants to learn to use his financial statements for finding treasure? If the net check is recorded as wages and the amount remitted to the authorities is recorded as taxes, where are the garnishments, health insurance payments, 401k's and FSA's recorded?

It is exceedingly difficult to manage these accounts if you don't know how much you are paying for them. Let's consider health insurance. Most employers have some sort of health insurance plans for their employees where at least a portion of the premium is paid by the employee through a payroll deduction. If the bookkeeper incorrectly books the payroll without the employee's portion of health insurance, how will the owner know the true cost of the employees or the true cost of the company portion of the insurance? Maybe more importantly, will he know if some of the employees are not contributing their share due to fraud or error?

Payroll Expenses Are Lumped Together On The Income Statement – Much of the content of this book focuses on understanding the differences between variable and fixed costs and how to calculate and manipulate margins. Some business owners do a pretty good job of segregating raw materials or job materials and reporting them in the cost of sales section of their profit and loss statement, but I find that most do not take the next step of segregating labor in this way. Labor is one of the largest expenses for almost any business owner, and yet, I rarely find it categorized correctly or properly analyzed. The margin reported on a profit and loss statement is useless if all wages are reported as fixed costs.

Other Variable Costs Are Lumped In With Fixed – Freight costs, if they are significant and recorded incorrectly, can skew the margin on a profit and loss statement. Freight costs are considered direct costs and should be reported as a cost of sale.

Personal Expenses On The Profit And Loss Statement – Personal expenses get in the way of true analysis of the financials. As discussed in another section, many business owners mistakenly believe that blurring the line between personal and business expenses is a great tax strategy and will result in greater business success. Personal expenses on the company books only skews the numbers and makes analysis cumbersome and prone to error.

Bank Reconciliations Are Not Performed – Some of my clients are greatly relieved when I help them work out some of the little kinks in their business that helps them increase their profitability. Others don't even know how much money they have and are thrilled just to know that their bank accounts are reconciled! That's right, a lot of small businesses do not reconcile their bank accounts, or, if they do, there are so many "uncleared" items that they still aren't quite sure what the balance should be even after the "reconciliation" is completed.

Equipment Purchases Are Expensed – Certain purchases are capital assets, meaning, they are meant to last more than a year, and they are not sold in the normal course of business. Because they benefit more than one period, depreciation is calculated, and the expense is applied over the life of the asset. In many small companies, I find these purchases classified incorrectly – equipment is expensed rather than capitalized.

Sometimes, there is a fine line between an asset and an expense. For example, a laptop may be expected to last a few years, but it only cost $500. Is it worth the extra trouble and expense of capitalizing and depreciating? To address these issues, businesses should create policies that address the capitalization of purchases, naming which types of purchases should be capitalized as assets and which should be expensed, and create a spending threshold, so that purchases can be categorized uniformly.

Loans Are Not Set Up, Or Are Set Up Incorrectly When equipment is mortgaged, or when an organization incurs any other type of loan, a liability should be set up on the balance sheet. As payments are made, the loan should be reduced by the principle, and interest expensed in the period incurred. Commonly, the bookkeeper fails to set up a liability. As payments are made, they are recorded as debits against a liability that does not exist, and no interest is recorded. This creates errors in both the balance sheet and the profit and loss statement.

Chapter 12 – RANDY MARGINS MATTER

How one small business added $100,000 in profit through margin analysis

As you learn to utilize your financial statements to optimize the earning potential of your business, a good place to start is with one simple step. Stop thinking in terms of dollars and start thinking in terms of percentages.

If your accountant is not already doing so, have them add a column to every financial statement that shows you the relevant percentages. On a profit and loss statement (aka, income statement) you will generally have all items on the page shown as a percentage of gross or net revenues. In other words, it is very helpful to know what your total cost of goods is as a percentage of either gross or net revenues. Likewise, knowing your rent or payroll as a percent of revenues is more useful than knowing the raw numbers.

For an example of how helpful this can be, let's look at gross profit margin and net profit margin in this example enterprise.

Gross Profit Margin = (Revenue minus Cost of Goods Sold) / Revenue

For example, it might look like this on a simple statement:

			% of Net Sales
Gross Sales	$850,000		102%
Less Returns	(15,000)		-2%
Net Sales		$835,000	100%
Cost of Goods Sold			
Product Purchases (assuming all purchases sold)	75,000		9%
Direct Labor	300,000		
Freight in Products	25,000		3%
Total Cost of Goods Sold		(400,000)	-48%
Gross Profit		$435,000	52%

Let's dig in on the idea. You sell apples at the Farmer's market. You can buy the apples for 25¢ each on most days. You usually sell them for 50¢. You can determine your "sales margin" by dividing 25/50 or 50%. But life isn't that easy. Some days you have to pay 30¢ due to shortages, and other days you find the suppliers all competing for your business and you negotiate a 20¢ cost.

In similar fashion at the Farmer's Market, you have days with no competition, and other days you have two other apple vendors in your same block. So, your sales price fluctuates. You keep track of all revenues for the month and find that you have $10,000 in sales. You keep all your receipts from purchases and find that you have paid $5,500 for the apples. You subtract this from total revenue of $10,000 for a net profit of $4500. You divide this by revenues to show your gross profit margin is 4500/10,000 or 45%.

Now you have certain costs. The rent of your space is $500 a month. Your truck expenses are $600. You pay a helper $1000 a month. For simplicity sake, we will say these are all of your expenses related to the sales of apples. Your total overhead is $2100. You subtract this from your gross profit of $4500 to find your net profit before tax of $2400. To determine your net profit percentage, you divide 2400/10,000 and you have 24%

By setting up that special column on your P and L (Profit and Loss) to see everything as a percentage of total revenues, you can also quickly see that your rent is 5% of revenues, your payroll is 10%, etc.

The margins that are most critical to manage:

Sales Profit Margin – Profit on sales of any specific product or group of products /Revenues on sales of those same items

Gross Profit Margin – Gross Profit/Total Revenues

Net Profit Margin – Net Profit/Total Revenues

You might also want to know your net profit margin including taxes.

Here is a P & L Statement that shows one method of laying out this information. You will see that you can easily tell the percentage associated with each and every cost of doing business.

Sales	Products	850,000.00	
	Less Returns	-15,000.00	
Total Sales		835,000.00	
Total COGS		400,000.00	47.9%
Gross Profit		435,000.00	52.1%
	Rent	60,000.00	7.2%
	Advertising	30,000.00	3.6%
	Telephone	3,000.00	0.4%
	Office Expenses	8,000.00	1.0%
	Payroll	100,000.00	12.0%
	Owner Payroll	100,000.00	12.0%
	Payroll Taxes	14,000.00	1.7%
	Bookkeeping and Accounting	5,000.00	0.6%
	Miscellaneous	3,600.00	0.4%
	Utilities	3,000.00	0.4%
Total Expenses		326,600.00	39.1%
Net Profit		108,400.00	13.0%
Taxes		1,400.00	0.2%
After Tax Profit		107,000.00	12.8%

Your small business may very likely be a sole proprietor, partnership, LLC, or Sub S corporation. In all of these cases, income will pass through to you and your partners or shareholders, resulting in a taxable event for every investor. In those cases, you may prefer to set aside a portion of your income for distributions to ensure that there is enough revenue distributed to pay the taxes. You might call this estimated tax distributions.

Of course, you hope that it is possible to make additional distributions above those needed to merely pay the tax consequences to yourself, partners, or shareholders, but at a minimum you want to plan for enough to cover everyone's tax liabilities.

REVIEW: In order to analyze your financial statement, you want to see both the gross amounts in dollars, but also the percentages. The percentages will allow you to compare your business with industry standards, will also provide an easier snapshot of any improvements, and will help you set budgets and goals. Since income revenues are always changing, seeing the raw dollar amount loses meaning. The percent amount is your key indicator to shoot for.

Chapter 13
MARGINS MATTER PART 2

Going from $0.00 Personal Income to $100,000 per Year

Robert bought a sporting goods store three years ago. So far, he hasn't been able to take any pay for himself. His wife is asking, "Is this a business or a hobby?" This is probably a good question for every business owner to ask. If you aren't earning the kind of money that you could earn at a job, is there a part of your business that is really a hobby?

In a small business you are likely working more hours and under more stress than you would be working for a boss. In addition, you are putting capital at risk. You may have borrowed from family, friends, banks, and credit cards to provide this opportunity. Your family has every right to wonder why there isn't more benefit to them from their sacrifice.

In Robert's case, the answer was relatively simple. He did need to increase sales, but that wasn't the biggest issue. His sales were close enough to $1,000,000 that we will just call it that for this example. However, a quick look at his Profit and Loss Statement and the actual big issue jumped off the page. His gross margin from sales was only 37%. The industry average was 45%, and some in his business were reaching 50% margins.

On $1m in sales, a difference in margins between 37% and 45% or 8% would yield additional income of $80,000 a year. Since Robert was just about at break even, this would mean taking home $80,000 a year to his family. If he were to use best practices that some in the industry were using, he could get another 5% and now he is making a respectable $130,000 for his effort. This increase comes without adding a single dollar to sales or overhead!!

Your margins are determined by a long list of issues, but let's look at the top four:

1. Selling Price

2. Purchase Price
3. Mix
4. Shrink

Robert started with what seemed to be the easiest place to attack; selling price. He had a meeting with his sales staff and made it clear that the discounting of product had to stop. The salespeople were being out negotiated by the customers, and the shop had a reputation for quickly discounting to get the deal. The new policy would be that all discounts had to be run through the owner.

When Robert looked at his P & L the next month (this is why getting statements out quickly matters), he saw an increase of 2% in margin. He dug a little deeper and saw that discounts were still happening. He decided to put in a bonus plan that paid out to his sales staff based on the overall margin for the shop's sales.

At the end of the second month, he found that margins were now up to 41%. His bank account was starting to show some growth.

Now Robert reviewed purchasing. Was he getting the best deals, or had he become lazy and started to trust his suppliers too much? You see, it is the unusual supplier who is going to give up their margin unless you ask for better pricing. In fact, you may need to bring in competitors and challenge every cost. You may be able to increase margins by buying larger quantities, taking advantage of deals, and looking for closeout offers. Robert dug in and found his margins increased another 2% due to better buying tactics.

Next, Robert tackled the product mix. Some items had 35% margins based on the manufacturer's suggested prices. Other items had 50% margins. Some had even higher margins. He sat down with the staff again to discuss how their bonuses would be increased if they would sell more of the 50% margin products.

When the next P & L came in, Robert was thrilled to see that his average margin was now at the industry standard. He had one more place to find some additional profit. That was in shrink.

Shrink effects margins in two ways. One is theft. The other is obsolescence. Robert created a new inventory data base and carefully evaluated what was and wasn't selling. You see, *companies who sell products often become museums of stale products.* Robert put on a huge sale to move out old products that weren't selling. This created a huge cash influx that he could now use to buy specials or larger quantities of items that were selling well.

His next P & L had a bit of a shock. His margins went back down again. Of course, this was a one-month blip due to his having sold so much old product at a discount. With a clean inventory, he should start to see improvements in the next month.

Robert also took a look at procedures that might reduce shrink from theft. He found articles in his trade magazine that showed more theft came from employees than customers. So, he evaluated ways that would attack both of these possible problems.

Over the next few months Robert was able to consistently hit 45% margins, and he continued to work hard on purchasing. The result of freshening his inventory and training his sales force had a side benefit. Sales went up, too. Robert is a perfect example of paying close attention to his financial statement month-by-month and creating over $100,000 per year in additional income for his family.

Next chapter, we will look at how carefully evaluating the P & L for overhead and other costs can also make a marginally successful business into a great asset.

Chapter 14
FINANCIAL REPORTS REVEAL LUXURIES

A Very Personal Lesson

"Do you like luxuries?" This was the startling question put to Andrew by his outside business consultant.

"Not really," Andrew responded, defensively. "I've kind of gone through that phase of my life and am trying to be more down to earth in my tastes."

"Well then," wondered the consultant out loud, "Why are you spending so much of your company money on luxuries you don't need and can't afford?"

Andrew had called in the consultant because his company was in serious trouble. He was taking out a nice salary, but not a luxurious one. Sales were about the same as last year, but profits had turned to losses, and cash was drying up quickly.

"Like what?" Andrew asked, truly wanting to know.

The consultant proceeded to list about $90,000 of annual overhead that wasn't really contributing to the bottom line, and that seemed to the consultant to be potentially expendable. $90,000 a year would quickly right the corporate ship and create positive cash flow.

How did the consultant find the culprits? He compared prior year financial information to the current year, paying close attention to every overhead item. It was quickly apparent that payroll overhead was up $40,000. This turned out to be two new positions that hadn't existed in the prior year. The consultant didn't even have to ask what these new hires did for the company. They hadn't been necessary in the past with similar sales volumes, they had not helped sales go up or contributed to increased margins or decreased overhead in other categories. They were almost by definition, a luxury.

Next, there were new expenses for trade shows. $15,000 represented a new show that the company had not participated in before that year. This was not as obvious a luxury. Did it bring in new business? Was it bringing in enough new business and/or clearly have the potential to bring new business that would justify the time, energy, and expense?

Each line item was also appraised to see if there were opportunities to reduce expenditures that had been in place for years. Were there new technologies, new suppliers, or new methods to achieve needed results with lower costs. One such opportunity showed up in the accounting department.

The company was large enough to justify a full-charge bookkeeper/IT person. This position oversaw clerks who input orders, handled purchase order processing, etc. The position also maintained other aspects of the accounting and the computers and software needed to run the department.

This department had an assistant bookkeeper. This position was for payroll and creating month end statements, making tax deposits, and other similar tasks. The consultant suggested that this position could be outsourced to a payroll and HR company who was far more efficient at these types of tasks. They would get better results for a fraction of the expense.

Finally, the consultant pointed to the inventory. The company was only turning its inventory 2X per year. In their industry, the norm was 4X per year. The cost of maintaining twice as much inventory as their competition was enormous. Those costs included space rent, cost of funds, shrinkage, and insurance.

All of these issues could be seen from reading financial statements. A few hours of work resulted in saving the company $90,000 a year and making them more efficient going forward.

Next, we'll take a look at how a financial statement might help you get "real."

Chapter 15
FINANCIAL REPORTS REVEAL FANTASY THINKING

What's Your Fantasy?

The company was having a very good year, and Ashley was proud of herself and everyone else on her team. Finally, years of effort were paying off. The cash balances were growing along with sales. Ashley was thinking some well-deserved Christmas bonuses would be the perfect end to this year.

But something was gnawing in the back of Ashley's mind. There was a sense that it was all too good to be true. She had felt this way much earlier in the year but had dismissed the feelings. Why spoil the party? It is against the business owner's creed to go looking for trouble. (sarcasm alert)

The mail she got at home shocked her. It was from the IRS. The reason for the correspondence was the company was behind in employment tax deposits, and did she know she was personally liable for any shortages. She didn't sleep that night, waiting for a chance to check with her bookkeeper the next day.

"Why are we behind on employment taxes?" she asked, the blood rushing to her cheeks. "There is plenty of money in the checking account."

The bookkeeper couldn't even look her in the eye, "We missed a payment way back in January. It was my fault. I didn't remember to send the payroll taxes. I was afraid you'd fire me if I told you. Then the next one came due and we didn't have the funds to pay both, so I just let that one slide also."

Ashley was afraid she was going to pass out from rage. "I thought we were having a great year, "she fumed. "Where is our current income statement and balance sheet?"

"I haven't done one for months," the bookkeeper murmured. "You haven't asked, and if you'd seen the statements, you might have figured out the issue. I wasn't going to slit my own throat."

Great companies insist on seeing an income statement and balance sheet at least once per month. We suggest a flash statement on the 5th business day, and a final reporting by the 15th. The bookkeeper in this scenario was probably correct. If the owner had wanted to be sure the growing bank account was due to profits and not some anomaly, she could have checked the financials. The growing amount in employment taxes due would have triggered the critical questions.

The best solution to this issue would be to hire an outside payroll processing company. These two tasks are inefficient when handled by employees compared to the reasonable fees charged by various payroll firms. The tax deposits would have been made automatically. In addition, most of these companies guarantee that your tax information will be prepared on time, so that your tax deposits can be transferred on time, using an automatic system.

This example case of fantasy thinking is not unique to payroll taxes. It is easy to have great cash in the bank due to decreased inventory, increased payables, or better collections of receivables. None of these have anything to do with profits but might create a false sense of good times.

For instance, maybe Ashley's problem wasn't payroll taxes. Maybe two of her suppliers had gone from COD to 30-day terms. Maybe the total outstanding for just these two suppliers had gone from $1,000 to $30,000. You see, that would be the same as getting a $29,000 loan. It isn't profit, it is just a cash flow benefit.

Or, maybe Ashley had created a special on her top selling product, and the inventory on that item had gone from $40,000 to $20,000 as shipments increased, but the new supplies had not yet reached the company. That is the same as cashing in $20,000 in stocks or bonds to run the company. Just a cash flow benefit, not profit.

These things also work in reverse. Ashely might have been singing the blues because cash in the bank was under $2000 and she liked to keep it up around $25,000. She goes to bookkeeping to complain that there are unexpected losses. The bookkeeper explains that two major clients have fallen behind on payments by about $20,000. This is as if Ashley had loaned out $20,000. This is not a loss, but just a cash flow issue. Obviously, Ashley needs to take action, but she doesn't need to fret about a structural loss. If those receivables become uncollectable, that is another story.

Here's an idea. Figure out the most critical metrices of your company and have those reported daily. You may find you could run your company from Maui. The next chapter is all about KPI or key performance indicators.

Chapter 16
KPI

The Six Numbers You Need to Run Any Business

How would you like to run your company from anywhere in the world where you can get dependable Internet access?

If you have a business that is a "going concern," (no threat of bankruptcy) and if your specific labor is not required in order for the product or service to be generated, you should be able to run that company by simply reviewing certain numbers each day. The numbers are a bit different for each company, but they come down to the same thing. These numbers are known as key performance indicators or KPI. You may have heard them referred to as metrics. They are commonly compiled on a dashboard.

First, what is a going concern? That is a business that has sufficient revenues and profits to pay the overhead, and enough cash flow to maintain the lines of products or services that sales depend upon.

Once your company has reached that point, you should be able to hire folks to handle all the daily needs, including a CEO and CFO depending on the size of the company. For a small company, you might need a talented and honest general manager, and a solid outside accountant or CPA.

With all that in place, you merely need the accountant to send you six numbers each day/week/month. From those numbers you will be able to determine if you are staying the course or improving, rather than losing momentum or hitting bumps in the road that could do damage. Here are some examples from which to draw your own specific six numbers. More follow at the end of the chapter.

1. Sales. Obvious right? You will be amazed at the number of business owners who **don't track sales**. Sales should be tracked daily, then compared to same period last year, and even back many years. The sales number should be net of any discounts, returns, and/or

credit card costs. The first number I want to see is sales by day, month-to-date, year-to-date, and **compared** to prior years and the current plan.

2. Gross profit margin. After all costs are computed that are required to produce the above sales, the remaining money is the gross profit. I want to see this number as a percent of the first number. Included in this number is cost of goods, freight in, shrink, and labor related to the production of the goods or service (not overhead). This number should also be reported daily, month-to-date, year-to-date, then **compared** to prior years and the current plan.

3. Overhead. For almost all businesses, this is everything else. All costs related to the day-to-day operation of the business. Salaries, rents, commission, utilities, etc. Generally, this isn't a number that needs to be updated daily and would require a lot of extra work to do so. For daily and weekly purposed, compute a daily overhead

amount based on either the prior month or the budget for the current month.

4. Net profit. If you only want 5 numbers per day, you can eliminate this one. This number is implied by the combination of the first three. You may want to set a profit per day goal and use this metric as a way to spot trends.

5. Inventory Turns. Most good computer systems today should be able to keep track of inventory by the day. Anything sold is immediately subtracted. Any new product being purchased is immediately added when checked in by receiving. I would want to see this number as a percentage of sales and/or better yet, converted into annual turns. With sales today and today's inventory, how many times per year am I turning my inventory. I want to know this by day and year-to-date. There should be a budgeted number that you are trying to meet or exceed.

6. Cash Flow. There are many ways to create a cash flow analysis. I suggest that you determine an amount that you want to have in the bank; say $20,000. You take today's bank balance, subtract all outstanding cash requirements for the next 30 days, add estimated cash income for the next 30 days, and determine if you bank account will remain above $20,000. If this number is generated daily, it will not be necessary to set up a more complicated approach.

7. Open to Buy. An alternative to #6 would be using an open-to-buy system. Purchases of product related to cost-of-goods would need to be the same or less than cost-of-goods sold for any period. The number you would want would merely be that ratio above or below even (e.g. +10% or -22%).

In order for this system to work really well, your team should create budgets for all of these numbers, and sub budgets for some of them. If good budgets are in place, it would be possible for you to merely receive a report with a single word or number representing the daily, weekly, or month-to-date comparison of the budget to reality. You would only dig into the numbers if the budget was off significantly.

Another preparatory number that should be in place is the break-even analysis by day, week, and month. If you divide the overhead by the gross margin %, you will get sales necessary to break even. In other words, if your gross margin is 45% and your overhead is $25,000 per month, you monthly breakeven is $55,555. If you are open every day, divide by 30, and you need $1852 per day to break even. After that comes profit.

Another trick is to build you desired profit into the break-even analysis. In the above example you could add $4000 as your desired profit. Now your daily goal is $2148 as long as the other numbers stay in budget.

All of these numbers are easily computed and can be updated in real time if you have a good computer system and use a quality accountant or CPA to prepare the formulas, spread sheets, and reporting methods

The numbers by themselves are not magic. It will be your job, as you lounge by the pool, to analyze those numbers, ask questions of those who are responsible, and expect them to make the corrections. If you are actually still running the business from your office, these numbers are still an amazing tool to help you sleep better at night, and to provide guidance as to where you should look for improvements.

There are many numbers that might be on this list that we didn't discuss yet. Some of those would include:

1. Accounts Receivable average aging
2. Accounts Payable average aging
3. Gross production numbers (manufacturing and services like lawyers, accountants, plumbers). How much did the factory produce? How many billable hours did professional staff or service technicians produce?
4. Backlog report – How many days of orders are backlogged waiting for product or services?

5. Backorder report – What percent of orders were shipped incomplete or late due to out of stock or late performance of services?

Next, we'll take a look at how financial information can call attention to an issue before that issue gets way out of control.

Chapter 17
WARREN BUFFETT

"Risk Comes From Not Knowing What You're Doing." Or You Can't Manage What You Don't Count

What company wouldn't be thrilled to see a doubling of revenue year over year? Triple would be even better! Most would be counting their blessings to see an average of 35% per year over many years. Certainly, such numbers would eventually provide the owner with fast cars, exotic trips, and a gold Apple Watch. Or Not!

Most companies that experience such growth are headed up by owners who have never done it before. They are completely inexperienced at the tasks that lay ahead. They have never had this many employees, this large of an accounts receivable or payable, this much of an outstanding loan, or this large an overhead. For the purposes of this chapter, we won't consider the huge issues surrounding knowing how to hire and train managers, or the even more difficult task of giving away responsibility or authority. We'll just stick to numbers.

(For more on managing a growing company, see Randy's book: When Friday Isn't Payday)

What Could Possibly Go Wrong?

Margins – When sales are exploding, supply lines might become strained or internal efficiencies will be sacrificed. There are many ways that cost per unit can go up as inexperienced staff is added, equipment is stretched beyond normal, and inventory management becomes sloppy. Shrinkage may increase due to dead products. (See the earlier information on margins in section 1 and 2.)

Any or all of these things might make a 5% or more difference in margins. Even a 5% drop could dry up profits or result in losses.

Solutions:

- Evaluate each new product to make sure that you at least take into account the potential effect of smaller margins compared to historic margins.
- Watch monthly stats on margins to catch slippage quickly.
- Get rid of items destined to become museum pieces fast.
- Evaluate the possibility of slowing your sales increases if supply lines or internal inefficiencies are hurting margins. Alternative: take the lowered margins into account in budgeting and planning.
- Increase prices to increase margins. Sales may suffer, but sales don't appear to be the issue

Accounts Receivable – If you are a manufacturer, wholesaler or other company that gives terms to your clients, increasing sales results in increasing receivables. Having more outstanding collections to manage increases the potential for those receivables to start getting older, and thus harder to collect. But, just in general, the amount of your loan to your customers is a drain on your capital.

Solutions:

- Get weekly reports on total receivables aging and specifically all accounts over 60 days.
- Budget the total % of sales that you expect to be in each aging category. Jump on any situations outside of budget.
- Give discounts to encourage early payment.
- Evaluate cash flow analysis to see at what point budgeted receivables will outstrip your ability to finance them.
- Fire customers that are not staying within terms. You hate to lose them, but the best time to trim the customer list of unprofitable business is when you are growing like crazy.
- Set up an accounts receivable financing line with your bank or other lender

- Take credit cards for payment from customers who pay with their order.

Inventory – One might think that getting too much inventory would never be an issue in the fast-growing company. That is partially true. The hot selling items are probably turning 12 or more times per year. But the problem comes with slow moving items or items that take a long time to arrive. It is easy to purchase a huge amount of product into the pipeline, and then have far fewer sales than expected on that item.

Even fast selling products could end up tying up a substantial amount of cash in raw materials, work in process, or product on the way. The cash may now be tied up in inventory and receivables, and the combination can be devastating.

Solutions:
- Budget inventory, including all product that is contracted for. Evaluate in terms of when payment needs to be made. Spread this out by month, and

budget what you believe you can afford to pay each month.

- If asset growth is outstripping available cash, cash will have to come from better terms on purchases, borrowing, and/or an infusion of equity.
- Maintain inventory budgets by line item. Cut purchases quickly as needed.

More like this in the next chapter.

Chapter 18
COUNT EVERYTHING

The In-N-Out Way

In-N-Out Burger should win the prize for best run business in the world. They should be teaching courses on how to manage businesses. If even 30% of US companies were run as well as they are, the GNP would skyrocket.

In-N-Out counts everything. I know personally of one young man who was moving rapidly up in management. One night he noticed that the lettuce was running low. He checked prior years statistics on how many burgers they were likely to sell the rest of that night, checked his stock, and decided it would be tight, but okay.

Later, he checked again, and came to the same conclusion. At 12:30 a.m. the store ran out of lettuce. 20 people didn't get lettuce that night. The young man was knocked off his management track and back to line status. He was told that he should have called his manager to get a second opinion. All this over 20 customers who didn't get lettuce on their burger.

What would happen in your business? Would anyone be checking the inventory that closely? Would anyone be able to review prior years statistics? Would anyone be demoted because 20 people didn't get their lettuce just before closing?

Maybe you think the situation above was over-the-top and unnecessary, but it has allowed In-N-Out to become a major regional chain still under private ownership.

Tracking Traffic

The owner of another business I know about complains that his sales are down. He always seems surprised. The reality is that his business is seasonal, and if he were tracking sales by the day or week or month, he could easily predict when he will be slow.

Benefits of tracking everything:

- Helps with staffing decisions
- Advertising could help to even-out the seasonal lulls
- Change the product mix or pricing based on season or

even time of day

- Plan cash flow based on slower or more robust seasons

Tracking the Source of Traffic

Most small business owners do some types of advertising. Most fail to keep track of results. It is the rare business that asks an obviously new customer, "How did you hear about us?" Rarer still would be keeping track of the responses in some detailed way.

Benefits:

- Determine what advertising and promotion is working
- See if you are getting referrals – reward those sending referrals
- Allows for inexpensive testing of new approaches to generate traffic

Tracking The Closing Ratio

The closing ratio can make or break any business. There is a cost of new customer acquisition. It might be $1 or $100 or even more. This is the average amount of money you spend through all means to get a customer to walk through the door. Costs could include a portion of rent that is paid for an amazing location, advertising, social media effort, community outreach, sales, signage and more.

If that customer walks through the door and you or your staff fail to close them on a purchase, your cost of acquisition is wasted. If you have three salespeople and one closes 80%, one closes 50%, and one closes 30%, every customer who is waited on by the third sales person instead of the first one, is costing you huge money. Do you keep track of your closing ratio overall and by salesperson? Imagine if your closing ratio went up 20%. What would that do to sales and profits?

Benefits:
- Determine an acceptable closing ratio
- Set commissions or other incentives based on closing ratio

- Create sales training and measure results
- Retrain or fire those who under perform

What should you be counting? This is a very, very short list of possible aspects of your business worth counting. Count:

- Contact information like emails, text numbers, collected each day
- Incoming phone calls by subject matter
- New reviews on Yelp and Google My Business
- Lost sales caused by out of stock – by item
- Customer count by hour
- Sales per customer
- Sales per invoice – dollar and units

In the next chapter we'll talk about how accounting can save you from your dumb mistakes.

Chapter 19
I INVENTED A WARNING APP

"That Was Really Dumb"

"There is an app for everything," is almost true. However, I could really use an app that gives me a buzz in my pocket or taps me on the wrist just before I do something dumb. This would be especially useful when it comes to financial decisions. You are just about to spend $75,000 on a Challenger Hellfire when "bing!"

I would imagine that such an app will be possible in the future, but the closest thing we have to such a great tool would be financial reporting systems. And it is possible to set up your systems to create warnings by the day or even by the minute.

For instance, you might have a policy regarding how much of a discount can be offered by your salespeople or customer service staff. When they try to process an order that has a greater discount, the software can be programmed to stop that sale unless a manager provides an override.

Or, maybe you create an open to buy system to limit purchasing too much product. You can set up your system to stop an order from being placed if it is outside the parameters that you have created.

Payroll can be monitored by the day or even tied to sales. If sales fall below a certain dollar amount for any given period, you can be notified. If payroll as a percentage of sales drops to a preset amount, you can be notified.

You might want to do a brainstorming session with your top managers or just with yourself to imagine the potential warnings you would like to set up for your system. The potential list would be in the dozens.

Here are other possibilities:

- Any of the KPI's mentioned in the chapter above
- Critical product inventory item or items dropping below preset number
- Purchase order being placed above some limit

- Payment being made above some limit
- Order being created for customer on credit hold
- Equipment or vehicle periodic maintenance missed

Chapter 20

Do You Know What Your Sales Were Last Year Same Month? The Year Before?

Do you like surprises? Not the kind where you open the front door to 50 of your best friends singing Happy Birthday. Not even the kind where you get an unexpected gift or honor. The kind of surprise you probably really don't like at all: dropping sales, lower traffic, less profit, shrinking margins, and especially dwindling cash.

In small business there are going to be plenty of surprises affecting all of these important elements. Economic conditions, weather, a new competitor, a bad Yelp review or two or three, and you can be faced with lower activity and even losses.

One great goal for any company might be to reduce surprises to a minimum. To some extent you may be able to do this by paying careful attention to national and regional financial news, industry trends and news, and asking a lot of questions of reps who call on you regarding local conditions such as new competitors.

You can reduce surprises by keeping accurate records of prior years, and then budgeting your expectations for the coming year. As noted in an earlier chapter on counting, you can count dozens of critical elements about your business, and then create budgets for each. For the purposes of this chapter, we want to drill down on the most important elements that should be watched carefully, and why.

Janet runs a motorcycle helmet distribution company. She knows that the business is seasonal with sales dropping way off during the last 4 months of the year, but she still runs out of money and gets behind in paying her bills every January. Her tax preparer can show her that the company is profitable, and she takes home a reasonable salary, but the cycle repeats itself every year. Just when she needs to buy inventory for the coming season, she is in a battle with her suppliers over her past due invoices.

Janet, like many other business owners, pays little to no attention to her financial statements, and makes no effort to budget. A few minor changes in her methods, much of which can be automated by a CPA, and she will solve this problem.

First, she wants to receive a sales analysis by month. This should show at least two prior years, preferably three. This is very simple to create, and the report might look like this.

	Jan	Feb	March	April	May	June	July	Aug	Sept	Oct	Nov	Dec	
2013	80000	72000	90000	120000	130000	150000	140000	140000	100000	80000	65000	75000	1242000
2014	85000	70000	95000	110000	140000	155000	140000	135000	120000	80000	70000	70000	1270000
2015	85000	75000	1E+05	105000	145000	165000	150000	140000	125000	75000	65000	70000	1300000

Next, she should ask to receive a very similar report on profits by month for the same period.

	Jan	Feb	March	April	May	June	July	Aug	Sept	Oct	Nov	Dec	
2013	-5000	-7000	1000	10000	12000	18000	15000	12000	5000	-8000	-20000	-10000	23000
2014	-4000	-8000	2000	5000	14000	17000	12000	15000	7000	-7000	-10000	-12000	31000
2015	-4000	-6000	6000	6000	15000	20000	16000	14000	8000	-5000	-2000	-4000	64000

Because she offers her customers payment terms, much of her cash from sales is delayed by 30 days or more. Therefore, she wants to have another similar report for cash receipts by month. This could also have a second report attached that would show cash receipts less overhead expenses by month. This will show cash flow other than purchases.

If she has reports that show her specifically what her cash shortfall is going to look like in October, November, and December, she can start to plan by lowering purchasing, increasing collection efforts, offering specials, and potentially laying off staff. This way she can squirrel away enough money to pay her bills during the lean months.

There is a much more sophisticated report called a cash flow analysis. This would take into consideration purchases, payables, and every other aspect of the business that impacts cash. But because it is sophisticated, it can be daunting to some users. By sticking with the simple reports above, almost anyone can see the trends and try to correct for them.

Janet could immediately see options that could help her through that tough spot each year.

- Reduce purchases earlier so that payment to suppliers would be paid by the time she needed to buy more.
- Reduce overhead earlier and more drastically so as to not use up funds during the waning sales months when the workload was too light for so many employees. This could be done by layoffs in slow times, or by using temporary workers in the better months.
- Get a line of credit to pay off suppliers
- Become much more aggressive about collecting accounts receivable during the end of the season, before things slow down for her customers.
- Build up a larger cash reserve by reducing some spending during the year. This reduction might come out of overhead or capital spending accounts. Don't buy any new computer systems or programs for one year.

Since Janet's payables problem was generally only about $100,000 (she owed $100,000 past due on her payables in January), she was able to solve this by cutting $20,000 in expenses during the year to build cash, reducing purchases early by $30,000 to reduce payables, increase collections of receivables by $10,000, and getting a line of credit for $35,000. She was still past due by $15,000, but this was manageable through working and communicating with her suppliers.

The next year she saved another $20,000 during the year and was in great shape going into the next season.

She figured her total time expense of reviewing the reports to be about 5 hours per year. Compare this to the hours of stressful calls dealing with angry suppliers who are demanding payment before shipment.

Chapter 21
SERIOUSLY

Where Did All My Cash Go?

Your CPA says you have to pay a bunch of taxes because of your great profits. Multiple emotions flood your brain. **Great!** We are finally making the kind of money we knew this company could generate. **Ouch!** The taxes are huge. Not only do I have to pay all those taxes for last year's sales, but I also have to pay the first quarterly installment based on those profits. It is a huge number. **Sigh!** Lots of taxes to pay, but with all those profits, I should have plenty of money to pay them on time. **Agghhh!!** There is no money. In fact, there isn't even enough money to run the company effectively. How will I pay the taxes?

It is not unusual at all for profitable companies, especially growing companies, to run out of cash. The reason is simple, though often not understood by owners: profits can be consumed by inventory, receivables, and capital expenditures. The income statement will show a profit, but the profit is tied up in increasing assets.

As we have been pointing out in Sections 1-9, business owners can avoid surprises, and increase profits, cash, or at least anticipate cash issues by having a working understanding of their financial statements. There are several ways to watch cash.

Cash Flow Analysis

A proper cash flow analysis is a sophisticated financial report that anticipates cash inflows and outflows based on historical trends, including average days to be paid on receivables, and average days to pay payables. This analysis also takes into consideration inventory flows based on the timing of new inventory coming in and historical information regarding sales. What this report cannot take into consideration are anomalies such as:

- Dramatic swings in sales by product or category. If you start to accumulate a lot of slow-moving inventory and are running out of good product, this will result in cash shortages that won't be picked up on a cash flow analysis.
- Creeping bad debt. If your receivables are not getting paid on time, and/or you have some debt that is uncollectable, this will not show.
- Major unbudgeted capital expenditures on new equipment or major upgrades or repairs.

A cash flow analysis will show you where to anticipate shortfalls in your cash, and some companies use this analysis to invest amounts not currently needed in short term securities.

Balance Sheet Comps

Running monthly, quarterly, or annual balance sheets side by side can quickly show you trends in categories such as outstanding payables, receivables, or cash, inventory, etc.

When running the comps, you might also want to show each category as a percentage of the parent class, either assets or liabilities. This way, if inventory is increasing as a percent of total assets, you will see that number jumping out at you.

You can also ask for a change in position report. This will provide you with changes by dollars or percentages for each category on the balance sheet.

Exception Reports

A great favorite for owners who have no time or desire to analyze the reports is the exception report. Here you set budgets for everything. Take inventory as an example. You could set the inventory budget to be no greater than $100,000 or if the company is growing, you could set inventory to be no more than 15% of assets. Another possibility is that the inventory would be a percentage of sales. You could even set it to show no more than and no less than. Now, when the trigger is hit, you are notified, and you can speak to your buyer to make sure that they either increase or decrease purchases accordingly.

Your bookkeeper should be able to do these reports from any basic system like Quickbooks. If they aren't able to figure it out, check with your CPA. They may be able to set it up for you in such a way that your bookkeeper can keep the system up to date.

I want to give a huge shout out to CPA Shaila Chamberlain who helped me with editing this material. She made a huge contribution to making this difficult content easier to read and understand. Shaila operates a CPA firm in the Riverside/Corona area of Southern California. You can reach her at 951-768-2969. Of course, she is also the co-author of this book, and we turn the mic over to her for the following chapter.

Chapter 22 - SHAILA

Why Choosing a Great Bookkeeper/Accountant/CPA Matters

I'm a bookkeeping nerd. Why? Because everything, everything you've read in this book will not make a bit of difference if your bookkeeping is shoddy. **Garbage in...garbage out**.

"Not me," you say. "I pay someone to keep my books."

This really doesn't matter at all. There is no "universal" test for bookkeepers. Anyone can call themselves a bookkeeper, accountant, controller or even chief financial officer.

"Well," you say, "I have a CPA prepare my taxes. He will make sure that my books are in shape."

Wrong again! Next time you have your taxes prepared, you should try reading the engagement letter. It clearly states that the CPA is under no obligation to fix your bookkeeping. And really, when is the last time your CPA contacted you after the fact and gave you some tips on recording your transactions correctly?

"What difference does it make, really?" you ask. "I just need my financials for tax purposes anyway."

Way, Way, Way wrong!

If you've learned anything from this book, financial information matters. How can you speed up your cash inflow if you have no clue what your receivables balance is? How can you know if your debt to equity ratio is strong enough to get a line of credit if you don't know your debt or equity? Besides, mistakes in your bookkeeping mean that revenues and expenses are wrong. Guess what? When your revenues and expenses are wrong, you pay the wrong amount in taxes!

So, how do you know if your bookkeeping is a problem? Here are 5 signs:

1. Negative numbers – There are a few exceptions, such as Accumulated Depreciation and Sales Returns and Allowances, but overwhelmingly, accounts should have **positive balances**. Particularly, negative balances in your accounts receivable, accounts payable, loan balances, sales or expenses point to trouble. A good accountant or bookkeeper will see this immediately and ask questions.

2. Run aging reports – An accounts receivable or accounts payable aging report breaks down your receivables and payables into 30-day chunks. Aging reports with balances in the 'current' column or '30-60 day' column generally mean that your invoicing and bill pay functions are being input correctly. Check for multiple entries in the 'over 60, 90 or 180 day' columns. Are

these true receivables or payables? Check again for negative balances. Unless credits have been issued, there should be none.

3. Look for interest expense – If you've purchased equipment or autos, or if you pay by credit card, there should be interest booked each month. No interest expense likely means that the transactions are not being recorded properly.

4. Undeposited Funds – When inputting a bank deposit, is the software prompting you to include payments that have already been deposited?

5. Uncleared checks – Check out your last bank reconciliation. Under "uncleared" items, are there checks more than 90 days old? Deposits more than 2-3 days? Any direct debits or credits? If so, your bank balance is most likely wrong.

Organize Your Financial Statements

Almost any financial software will organize your financial statements **to a point**. It's up to you to make them super-relevant to you. For example, if you have 5 different revenue streams, you may want to create a revenue account for each one. If you have different projects and would like to track profitability separately, you can use the 'location' or 'class' functions. Make sure all direct costs are included in Cost of Sales. Track Wages and Salaries by department or differentiate between Admin and Sales. Make the financial statements relevant to your business. Track in such a way that you can see and understand the data and use it to propel your business forward!

A Word On Taxes:

Universally, everyone hates taxes, and everyone thinks they should pay less. It's true: Uncle Sam wants our last buck and will do anything to get it. The way the tax code is written doesn't do us any favors. It encourages businesses to spend money to lower taxes. Sometimes, we are tempted to do all kinds of crazy things to limit our taxes, like push a lot of personal expenses into our business accounts. I've had clients who expense a Big Mac every day of the year and call them "client meetings". I've had clients take their families to the Bahamas on "business" trips, claiming that they are scouting locations for possible expansion. I've had clients who "network" at Disneyland. Unfortunately, most of these clients never became truly successful. They fell into the trap of limiting their success by limiting their taxes.

The problem is that mucking up our financial statements with personal expenses does not give us a true picture of our business success. It does nothing to help us chart our path toward greater and greater profitability. It only confuses us and encourages us to spend more and more money on unnecessary 'stuff'. Our tax code, whether inadvertent or not, encourages us to fail. For only by failing, can we truly limit our taxes.*

As my wise mother always told me, "Don't cut off your nose to spite your face!"

Use every business tax deduction you are entitled to, **if it makes business sense to spend the money**! If it doesn't make sense, outsmart Uncle Sam and keep your money in your pocket. There are savings vehicles and investments that are tax free or are deferred to a later period. Take advantage of those instead.

Finally, Learn as much as you can.
This book is a great start, but your education should never stop. **Find a good professional**. Pay them a little more if you must, but this is a worthwhile investment in your business.

> ***Author's Note:** One bright note in recent tax legislation - The Tax Cuts and Jobs Act of 2017 included the 'Qualified Business Income' deduction.

Say what you will about the overall effects of the TCJA, but this piece of the legislation is very good for small business. It is one of the few tax laws on the books that encourages profitability. The calculation is quite complex, but under normal circumstances, a business owner can deduct up to 20% of profits on his/her individual tax returns. In other words, the more profitable the business, the larger the deduction.

Chapter 23 – RANDY
"HOW MUCH SHOULD I CHARGE?"

Various Methods for Establishing Pricing

There is nothing in business more critical than deciding how much to charge for your products or services. If you charge too little, you don't have enough gross profit to cover overhead, and you can be out of business. If you charge too much, you may find you have no one buying your product, therefore same result. If you are only a little underpricing the market, you will get the reputation of a discounter, which can be good or bad. If you charge a little over the market, you can be seen as "pricey," which can be good or bad.

For the purposes of this exercise, we are going to look at the part of the pricing structure that determines if you get to stay in business, and how you can determine this through accounting.

Let's start with retail: Most retailers keystone (charge double their landed cost). Landed cost includes the actual cost of the item, the freight if there is any, and any preparation to get the item ready to sell (building it, painting it, etc.) When you double the cost of something you are charging a **100% markup**. But if you talk of this in terms of margin, then you are dividing the sell price minus cost by the sell price. So, a $1.00 sell price - $.50 cost divided by $1.00 sell is a **50% margin. 100% markup is exactly the same as 50% margin.**

It is important to get this concept clear in your mind, as you will want to talk to suppliers, accountants and bankers in the correct way. Let's do another example. If you buy something for $75 and sell it for $100, you will have a 33% markup. 133% of $75 = $100. But the margin is ($100-75)/100 or 25%.

While the keystone is the typical method of pricing in a retail shop, there are many other possible ways to price.

In retail, your MSRP (manufacturer's suggested retail price) is usually available through the supplier's catalog. You may choose to price most of your products at or near the MSRP. However, you may find that some of these are unrealistic. Thus, you may decide to play with the price to see how consumers react.

Keystone in retail is generally true for items costing between $5 and $20.00. Below $5, most retailers are going to charge more than keystone. So, something that costs $1 might sell for $3 or more. Above $20, it is common for retailers to work on less than keystone. However, even on large ticket items of $1000 or more, most retailers need to keep margins between 35 and 40%. So the $1000 cost item would need to sell for $1000/(100%-35%) or $1538 to $1000/(100%-40%) or $1667.

Clothing items are generally offered at the beginning of the season at 66% margins or 3X the cost. This allow the shop to discount the items by 50% at the end of the season and still not lose money. There are generally more losses on soft goods, therefore requiring higher margins.

Food products vary all over the board, but there are some very specific rules. Bakery items are generally 66% margins or 3X cost. Pasta's are more commonly 4X cost. Steaks and other higher priced items maybe as little as 2X cost. Beverages and deserts can be 5 to 10X cost.

In the service business, the rule of thumb was 3X cost. You took the cost of employee wages and overhead plus any special machine or other costs and charged 3X that amount. The theory was that there was 1/3 for the actual cost, 1/3 for the overhead, and 1/3 for profit.

In doing some research on this subject recently, I found half a dozen different methods for determining costs of service. The most common was to check the competition and be in the ballpark of what they are charging. That sounds similar to MSRP (Manufacturer's suggested retail price). Others said to charge what the market will bear. That sounded like guesswork to me.

There were those who suggested accounting methods which backed into the profitability of the specific service. So, if you know your total fixed overhead, then you know how many gross profit dollars it will take to cover that overhead and make the company money.

For example, let's say I have fixed overhead (rent, utilities, etc) of $5000 a month. I want to make $3000 a month. Therefore, I need $8,000 profit dollars to do that. If I have billings of $20,000, and the labor costs me $12,000, I've accomplished my goal. My job as owner is to keep sales at $20,000 and make sure my staff continues to accomplish the work for $12,000.

Wholesalers historically made 25% margin. There may be some who still do so. I don't know any. The new formula is 35% margin.

Manufacturers commonly shoot for 5X cost to retail. This means an item costing $1, packaged, packed and ready to ship, will cost $5 at retail. This allows the dealer to make 50% and the wholesaler to make 35%, leaving the manufacturer with a profit of 37%. Most manufacturers prefer to make 50% overall from cost to invoice price. This has led many manufacturers to go around the wholesalers and sell direct to retail stores, or to even go around the retailer and sell direct to consumers on Amazon, eBay, Etsy, or in their own online or brick and mortar retail store (Apple and Tesla.)

By having some sales at 5X cost, it allows the manufacturer to average their margin up from 37% to a more livable 50%.

Some companies believe that they can ignore all of these suggested methods. You can be sure that these standards have come into place through the clear thinking of the best in the industry, and only change when circumstance require it. Competition forces these results to stay lower than they might go, and the realities of overhead costs keep them from dropping below the standards.

Of course, this is a primer on the subject, and there may be differences in your industry. Your association likely provides guidance, your suppliers can help you, and there are often books that go into detail on every slice of the business world.

Let's look at a couple of real-world examples.

Some new owners believe that businesses are ripping off the world through high prices. They will commonly open their doors with the belief that they can do just fine by charging much lower prices than the robber barons.

The Drama Costume Shop starts selling product, and since they are dramatically undercutting their competitors, the sales come flying in. With increased sales comes the need for more employees, more desks, more square footage, more of everything. At some point there is a need for some layers of management.

So, the normal average cost of goods in the costume sales business is 50%. They've only been charging a 25% markup, so they can charge "fair" prices. At the end of the month, they look at their results and they are very impressed with their sales of $100,000.

Their cost of goods was $80,000 (20% margin or 25% mark up.) This left them $20,000 for overhead, taxes, etc. The next line item was shrinkage (soiled items, returns, stolen product, and product that was never going to sell – the last one would usually take months to determine). Shrinkage was 3%. Then merchant services (credit card fees) added another 2%. That left $15,000.

Rent $3000, Employees $10,000 (including benefits), accounting $500, Internet and utilities $1000, office supplies $500 and now we are at break even. But there are still many costs to go. Depreciation, advertising, website, insurance, travel (trade shows), government fees and local taxes, and more.

So even at $100,000 in first month sales, this company is on the way to bankruptcy. Sometimes these types of businesses will continue to stay in business using OPM (other people's money.) Their suppliers give them credit, they use credit cards or bank loans, and they borrow money from or sell stock to friends and family. Everyone thinks this is a great company because the sales are so high. But it is very common that no one is paying any attention to the Profit and Loss statement. There's money in the bank, and the owners are paying themselves, too. But the money is not from profits. It is from borrowing.

At the other end of the street is a law office. The owner is highly skilled at this craft and he thinks he should be worth what the other companies in town charge. He sets his rate at $350 per hour for regular work, and $500 an hour for trial work.

He gets a few good clients, and he gives them great results. His reputation is solid, and the word gets out about his successes. He hires a few clerks to do some of the work and even finds a couple of ways to automate or outsource some activity. The clerks make $25 an hour, and the automation and outsourcing cost an equivalent of $5 an hour. At the end of his first year he has billed $1,000,000, and his total cost to produce these services is only $400,000. His other overhead is $50,000, so he is happy with his $550,000 In personal take home.

He sees that if he just finds more clerks and outsourcing, he can really make a killing. But at the end of the second year his revenue falls to $500,000 and he makes nothing, even loses a bit.

There were other lawyers in town that were happy to charge less than him, and there was no significant difference in outcomes. So, there was a shift by his clients to these lower cost shops.

His real cost of services was so low because of his clever use of outsourcing and automation, that he still could have made a huge profit with a lower selling price. His selling prices were based on his ego and not on the market.

Chapter 24
GETTING TO REAL COSTS

Many Surprises Here

Imagine how complicated it must be to figure the actual cost of a car or a smartphone. You have all of these parts, the labor, the shipping of parts, the depreciation of equipment used to make and assemble things together, the shrinkage, and even the space taken up by all of these parts, people and equipment. Then there's the research and development, testing, and so much more that must be divided up among anticipated production.

Your business probably isn't this complicated. So, I'll talk about my old business, the manufacturing of water bottles. Pretty simple. There are only three parts. The bottle, the cap, and the little poppet in the cap that stops or allows the water to flow.

There's raw material for each part. There's machine time to blow mold the bottle or injection mold the cap and poppet. There's wear and tear on the molds. There is the cost of color that is added to make each part black or white. But no color for clear. And there is labor to watch the machines and remove parts from the molds.

Then there is the labor to move the items from production to packaging, the labor to put the poppet into the cap, and the labor to put the cap on the bottle. At each stage there may be loss or shrinkage due to the discovery of bad parts. There is the cost of the box, and the small boxes go into master packs.

In order to determine the final cost of that bottle, packed and ready to go, each of these elements must be carefully determined.

One year, a particularly good year, we expected a very substantial profit. But when the books were delivered to my desk the profit was $200,000 less than expected. The hunt was on. You can be sure this was enough to get my attention.

Point number 1. If my accounting records weren't any good, it is unlikely that I would have ever found the culprit. As it was, even with very good books, the effort took real detective work.

The loss could have been anywhere, of course. It could have been higher than expected write off of accounts receivable. It could have been an increase in the cost of raw materials that had escaped our notice. It could have been an inventory write down due to incorrect counting or obsolete product. It could have been the result of office overhead being higher than budgeted.

But if your books are good, and you are watching these items monthly, most of these items would not escape your notice. Of course, it could have been $20,000 here and $30,000 there. The accounting staff looked. I looked. There was nothing we could find.

One day, I was looking at my sales management report. I wanted to see how our top accounts were doing and compare their sales and profitability in the just finished year compared to past years. As I looked down the top 20, I saw a new name.

A & B Plastics. They had never been in our top 100 customers and our sales to them had jumped up considerably from the prior year. Moreover, we didn't generally sell anything to other plastics companies.

I looked them up on the computer and checked their invoices. I was absolutely shocked to see that they had been buying our plastic scrap.

Let me explain. When you make a bottle or almost any plastic product, there is scrap. In the case of a blow molded bottle, there is quite a bit of scrap. The scrap generally goes into a shredding machine that grinds it up so that it can be recycled into the machine immediately.

There are some exceptions, and these exceptions get ground up, put into boxes and sold. What had happened is that the manufacturing employees on 2nd and 3rd shift had grown lazy, and they were putting good scrap into those boxes for resale.

The increase in scrap sales should have been caught by the shift supervisors, the department supervisor, and the CFO, but it wasn't. But it was caught by the accounting (in lowered profits), and by the reporting in the sales management reports.

Changes were made immediately. Daily accounting of all scrap was established, along with trigger points that would require a new evaluation of scrap rates.

This is how accounting is supposed to work. The accounting caught the issue, allowing management to manage the problem.

Let's take a look at a situation that came up last year with a service business. They were doing over $1,000,000 a year and everything was fine except for their $125,000 loss. A lot of detective work determined that:

- Some customers had not been invoiced for the work performed
- Discounts had been given on other work without management's approval
- Employees were booking hours as administrative that should have been billable

- Employees were often billing less than industry standard hours per shift

As a result of this, real costs were not being determined. Let's use the example of a front-end alignment. The employee charged with this task is able to do eight per day. He is paid $25 per hour and after all expenses related to his employment, his cost is $40 per hour. The company is charging $120 for that alignment.

However, if he only does six per day due to administrative time, his cost just went from $40 per alignment to $53. Now let's say that he loses the paperwork on one. His cost just went to $64 per alignment. It turns out that a lot of his buddies are coming here for alignments and he is giving them 20% off. Two of these jobs only bring in $100 instead of $120.

How could this go on for a year without it being discovered. Easy!! No budgets and no one looking at monthly income statements.

The first step in managing anything is to count it. The second step is to budget it. The third step is to compare actual results to the budget. You don't even necessarily need to wait until the end of the month to catch this one.

If the budget for the alignment department has been determined to be $960 per day, and the cost of labor is $320 per day, you can actually look at the numbers daily, weekly, or wait until monthly. It should never be less than once per month.

You see, in this case the total sales would have come in at $520 per day with labor still being $320. If the employee was required to capture administrative time, then labor would have been $240 with admin at $80. Pretty obvious problem here.

The manager checks to see if there were enough incoming sales to fill the day. Next, he checks to see if there were machine issues, major administrative tasks that needed more attention than usual, and whether the discounts were authorized.

If it turns out that everything was on the up and up, the budgets need to be changed. If it turns out that the employee was doing everything right, but this was unprofitable, then ownership can stop the discounts, cut the employee hours, and see if someone can do that admin who is paid $15 an hour.

Finding out your real costs can only happen when appropriate accounting methods are being applied, and when managers or owners understand how to analyze the books and find the underlying issues.

Chapter 25
INCREASING SALES THROUGH ACCOUNTING

Seriously!! Tracking sales by customer

In my experience, one of the biggest diamonds buried in the computerized files of any company is historic customer information. If you have fewer than 10 customers, and those customers tend to stay with you for many years, you can probably keep that historic information in your head. However, it is the rare company that has such an experience.

Most companies have dozens, hundreds, or even thousands of customers that have stopped doing business with them. Most companies have an equal number or more prospects that have never done business with them. And every company has customers whose sales have increased or decreased over the last months or years.

Are you looking at any of this data? Are you making any budgets that rely on this data? Are you comparing actual results to your plan on a regular basis? If not, you are missing huge opportunities for substantial increases in revenue.

I suppose the above is so obvious that it might not require unpacking for most readers. However, let's consider a few scenarios.

George runs a hair salon with five chairs. He has eight operators for those five chairs as he is open 12 hours per day and seven days per week.

Each chair has the potential for 12 clients per day, an average of one per hour. Some clients only require half an hour, some require two hours or more. Some visit the shop once per week, some twice a month, some every three weeks, and others once a month.

It would be impossible for George to keep track of all of these clients spending habits, so he has a sales-by-client report produced by his point of sale (POS) system. This allows him to see all the clients in various ways:

- Top down from spending the most to the least
- Dollars spent per hour from most to least
- Profit by client from most to least
- Sales by client by month alphabetically
- Sales by client by month by operator
- Operator total sales by day
- Operator total sales by hour
- Operator total sales by month

With this information George can see which clients bring the most revenue, the most profit, and/or the most revenue per hour. He can compare their sales by month to see if there is any increase or decrease, or even that the customer is no longer spending anything.

He also can check on the varying capabilities of his operators. George starts to see that one of his operators generates $50 of revenue per hour and $25 of profit, while his worst performing operator only generates $30 of revenue per hour and $15 of profit. This information will allow him to start asking questions and observing these different individuals to see why the big difference. This could result in training, encouragement, motivational tools, warnings, or termination for the lower performing person.

However, George notices that the better performer has many more clients who aren't coming in anymore. He is also able to see that a third operator has almost no loss of clients with $45 per hour of revenue and still $25 of profit, due to more product sales.

George finds that over the past three months, 20 customers have dropped to zero in sales. He calls each of them to find out why and to offer them incentives to come back again. Ten agreed to come back for another try. But more importantly, he learns that 15 of the 20 had the same reason for quitting the shop. The young woman selling product and setting appointments in the afternoon had been rude. One of the customers had even written about it on Yelp.

He also finds that he has 17 customers who are weekly visitors, who spend the most by far, and who have been coming to the shop for years. He decides to create a platinum club for those customers that includes special gifts, events, and discounts. He then encourages these customers to talk about the shop on social media and offers them incentives for any new clients they send to the shop.

Tracking Sales By Salesperson

In the above example, we saw a hint of the ideas of tracking sales by salesperson, as the operator would be a type of salesperson. However, when you have multiple sales professionals or sales rep agencies selling for you, there are many other metrics you may wish to track.

Many companies and/or sales managers are mostly interested in whether the salesperson is increasing sales. Total sales will be incentivized, quotas may determine their future with the company, and there may be competition between salespeople based on total sales.

However, there are many other ways to judge performance:

- New customers added
- Customer retention

- Profitability
- Lines added
- Specific product or services sold
- Specific promotions

Once again, these ways of measuring performance can have immense strategic importance.

Briana owns an insurance brokerage. She has five agents working for her. These are all seasoned agents, and each has 400 clients that they manage.

After instituting a program to keep track of the KPI's (Key Performance Indicators), Briana noticed right away that with the same number of clients, there were huge differences in sales, profitability, retention, and lines added. Moreover, the top agent scored highest in all KPI's and the worst agent was lowest across the board.

Briana had individual meetings with each agent and just listened to their methods before telling them about their standing. Then she brought up the standing and asked for each agent to identify any reasons that might account for the differences; no judgement, no criticism, and no training at this first meeting.

Armed with the stats and the conversations, Briana next held a brainstorming session designed to find ways to bring everyone up to the levels of the top performer. At this point, everyone was aware that there were now expectations of performance on these specific KPI's.

After the meeting, Briana instituted some of the ideas that were suggested, and she created some rewards for improvements. She also created some floors on each KPI. If any of the reps fell below the lowest acceptable number, there would be clearly spelled-out consequences, including termination.

Finally, Briana made sure that the top performer received public praise and special compensation bonuses for doing some mentoring.

Tracking Sales By Product Or Service

Phil owns a wholesale business. He sells a variety of products to retail stores and online. He carries about 1500 different SKU's (Stock Keeping Units). Some of those items have margins of 25%, some have margins of 35%. He also has items that he imports directly and those have margins of 66%.

All things being equal, Phil would like to sell more of those imported items. While it is true that there may be some other costs such as transit time, greater inventory on hand, and trips to Asia to ensure quality control, Phil still prefers to move more of these if possible.

Phil sets up a program that provides him with sales by item by month. He gets his first report back and finds that generally he is selling much more volume of the 25% items, the opposite of his intent. However, his top selling item is a 66% margin item and as he looks down the list, there is almost no clear way to see any trend at all.

Phil visits Ana, his top customer, and asks about the sales differences. She says that the imported items, in general, have had more defects. She also says that there are other products available to her that are almost identical for about a 10% lower price. The top selling item for Phil's company is also a big seller for Ana. She says that there is no real competition for that item.

Ana gets her marketing department together. They brainstorm on ways to differentiate the import products more along the lines of the top selling item. They consider making the other items in colors, bigger, smaller, changing the packaging, or dropping the price to be under the competition.

They then contemplate special spiffs for their own salesman to incentivize more emphasis on the higher margin items, deals for the customer, advertising to pull the items through the customer's clients, displays in the customer's place of business, and a huge bonus if the customer hits a sales objective.

Tracking Sales By Location, Territory, Country, And Industry

As a manufacturer, my company had sales in multiple industries in every state, and in about 30 countries on four continents.

By evaluating the sales by industry, we were able to determine how much to spend on trade shows, advertising, and new product development. In some cases, we might want to expand our efforts, in other cases, the trends suggested we spend almost nothing.

Our sales reports by country showed that every new item had a great start in Australia, but quickly peaked and started to decline. After a bit of an investigation, our customers there told us that garage manufacturers were copying our items and selling them for less, since they had no freight. We decided not to spend more money in Australia.

We also found that England, Belgium, and Germany loved our products, so we spent more effort in those countries.

Nationally, we determined that we were selling about the same across the US. However, logistically, we were better off selling locally. Since we had 20 million folks in our backyard, we started to concentrate the bulk of our sales effort in Southern California.

Tracking Profits By Customer/Salesman/Product

It is very easy to set up combinations of criteria for your sales reporting. You might find that one sales rep really likes a specific product or service and sells it like crazy. Another salesperson in another territory has their favorite. The same thing can be true of customers, as well.

In this case, it might be wise to have a sales meeting where the champions of various products can talk about their reasons for being such fans. Now the other salespeople might catch the vision and improve the sales of these items to their customers.

Chapter 26
FIRING CLIENTS THRU ACCOUNTING

Hard Choices

Some clients just aren't worth the trouble. Maybe they return products all the time. Maybe there is always a shortage on every shipment. Often there is a problem with paying on time. Others only buy your lowest profit items. Of course, there are those who don't buy much at all, complain, and pay late.

You can set up another combination of criteria to track these behaviors. But it may be simpler than that. You can check your Accounts Receivable aging to see if there are chronic slow pays. Determine what you consider to be the cut-off point. Now take a quick review of total sales volume and the type of products they purchase. Take your worst 5% and put them on notice.

Just because you put them on notice, doesn't necessarily say you'll stop doing business. Eventually they may need to be COD or even CIA (cash in advance). Some companies have one-time issues and otherwise pay their bills on time. Most slow pay accounts are chronic slow pay. For those, you may want to consider a full range of criteria as part of the decision to ease them out or just cut them off. Maybe they do a lot of volume. Maybe their purchases are very high margin items. The more valuable the account, the more reason to become creative in figuring out ways to lower your risks of default and costs of them being slow pay.

Another place to look for potential client firings is those who are your lowest 5% in terms of sales. Find out why they are doing such low volume. Do they have potential to improve? Are they buying high margin items? Do they cause any other type of issue?

Sometimes even large clients are not worth the trouble. Do a margin analysis. Who are your worst 20 clients by margin? For my plastics manufacturing company, Target was the culprit. We tried to renegotiate, but they didn't budge. They were 10% of our sales but the cost of doing business just wasn't worth it. We fired them.

On another occasion, we had a customer who was always claiming our shipments were short. The shortages were not just a few dollars but were significant. And every single shipment. We were not getting any such reports from other customers. We would carefully examine our freight documents. We could see no reason to accept the customer's version. However, we generally "gave in" to their demands for a credit.

After four or five such incidents in a row, we decided to take further action. We had their next shipment counted by five different members of the company. We took pictures as the material was loaded onto the pallets and the truck. Every box had a sequential number, and each pallet had its own documentation as to the box numbers on that pallet.

We sent the order and, to no one's surprise, we got the phone call complaining that, once again, we had short shipped. We now asked them to provide us with detailed pictures of the pallets and boxes. We asked them to review the sequential box markings and tell us which boxes were not in sequence. The company withdrew its request for a credit. We sent a firm letter indicating that we were removing them from our customer list.

Sometimes it isn't necessary to outright fire a client, you can just increase your price or make the terms less favorable. Sometimes these efforts will add enough profit to justify keeping the client. In other cases, they will self-select themselves to no longer do business with you.

Chapter 27
LITTLE THINGS MATTER

Why Great Managers Matter

Billy Beane understood that there are diamonds to be mined out of the balance sheet. In his case it was the balance sheets of hundreds of baseball players who had the potential to play for his Oakland Athletics. Beane (as in beane counter?) disrupted baseball's methods for evaluating players. In a game that is almost defined by its love of stats, Beane went looking for little things that mattered.

In the movie "Moneyball," the story is told of how Beane was required to cut payroll costs on the Athletics. He was able to do so and still field a team that was consistently competitive. He concentrated on items like the on base percentage rather than the more obvious stats like batting average or total home runs in a season. In doing so, he was able to hire players that were otherwise passed over, and therefore pay far less for each position.

In almost exactly the same way, business financial reports are made up of stats, and it isn't necessary to find a 10-carat stone to make a huge difference. The potential to dramatically change profits is often a combination of a bunch of .25-carat gems. That's how Beane did it.

The average small business might have at least 20 categories on the income statement that can be managed: Sales, discounts, credit card charges, cost of goods or services, rent, payroll, insurance, marketing, advertising, and so on.

Many owners pay a huge amount of attention to the sales number and go to a lot of trouble to increase sales. We will assume that the reason is ultimately to increase profits so that there is more take home pay for the owner.

We start with a company that has $100,000 in sales. Margins are 50%. So gross profit is $50,000. Overhead of all types is $40,000. So net profit is $10,000.

Let's assume a 20% sales increase would make everybody happy.

When you increase sales by 20%, you will also increase total cost of goods or services, and variable costs such as credit card charges, commissions, marketing expense, etc. Maybe the net profit before overhead will be around 20% of that total. 20% of an additional $20,000 in revenue increases profit by $4,000 in the example below

Sales	100,000	$120,000
		after 20% increase
COGS	$50,000 (50%)	$60,000
Variable costs	$30,000 (30%)	$36,000
Overhead	$10,000	$10,000
Profit	$10,000	$14,000

What if instead, the company stayed even in sales, but found an average 5% savings on all cost and overhead items. The savings would at $4,500 in profits (5% of the $90,000 total costs and overhead in the example.)

Sales	100,000	$100,000
COGS	$50,000 (47.5%)	$47,500
Variable costs	$30,000 (28.5%)	$28,500
Overhead	$10,000	$9,500
Profit	$10,000	$14,500

Is it easier to increase sales by 10% or cut costs by 5%? You may be able to do both. The issue here is that there are many ways to increase profits, and while increasing sales commonly comes top of mind, it is by no means the only way. In fact, there is a startling curve that many business owners often don't know about or fail to consider in planning. It works like this.

Let's consider the lemonade stand again. The sales are increasing and so are profits. First month is $1,000 in sales and $300 in profit. The only expenses are lemons, cups, and labor. Our 12-year old owner is maxed out at 15 hours per week and is making only $5 an hour for all the effort ($300 hours/60 hours or $5 an hour.) Moving to a better location seems like one way to increase sales and stay within 60 hours per month. But the new location requires $200 rent.

Sales increase to $1,500 and $450 in gross profit, but after the rent, profits are now only $250. Over the next few weeks, sales continue to increase to $2,000 a month with $600 gross profit and a $400 net. An employee is added to increase total hours to 120, but the employee needs to make $10 an hour X 60 hours or $600. Sales increase to $3,500 with $1,050 in gross profit, but after $200 rent and $600 payroll, the profit is now only $250. As the location becomes better known, sales increase to $5,000 with a $1,500 gross profit, and now there is a $700 net profit. Due to the total sales being higher, the lemons and cups can be purchased at lower prices, adding another $100 to profits.

This is a very typical sales/profit curve for any business of any size. New products, new locations, new employees, increased advertising, and other factors create dips in the expected earnings even when sales are improving. Meanwhile, sales increases often decrease costs due to efficiency.

These kinds of changes don't have to be a surprise. You can create forward looking spread sheets where you can plug in anticipated increases in expenses or decreases in costs related to improving sales. Have your accountant or CPA create an income statement by month that is interactive, so that as you change a value, it changes other relate values.

Chapter 28
FINANCIAL STATEMENTS

Key to Getting Best Price When You Sell Your Business

Dan is ready to sell his pizza joint. He's been at it for 30 years and he's ready to go fishing. The business has been good to him and his family. They have made a nice living, paid for a house, and set aside a nice retirement. But he needs a good price for the store to make the retirement secure. He calls a business broker.

The broker asks about his profits for the last three years. Dan really doesn't know what his profit was. The broker wants to know what he takes out of the business. Dan tells him his salary and benefits. The broker tells him that most pizza places sell for about three times the profit, which includes adding back the owner's compensation. In other words, the profit shown by the company will matter a lot. Every dollar of profit is worth $3.

Dan calls his bookkeeper and asks for a copy of the profit and loss (also known as an income statement.) He was shocked, sort of, to find out there was no profit. Using various approaches, his tax preparer had worked to keep his taxes low. The benefit when paying taxes turned into a liability when trying to sell.

The broker explained to Dan that he should take at least six months to as long as two years to build up his profit on the books. This would mean reversing all those tricks for a while. Dan had not really paid much attention to his financial statements over the years, so the accountant explained the process.

Dan had been very aggressive on things like car allowances, and some overhead items were a bit questionable. Business trips that had a vacation component, and dinners out that may or may not have had any business purpose, were other areas to report differently.

When Dan changed the way he reported his income, the profit went from -0- to $35,000 per year, giving Dan an extra $105,000 towards his retirement fund. Dan's only regret was that if he had been paying more attention to his financials, he may have been able to get the business on the market 6 months earlier.

Case study: A nail salon was also making $0 when the owner decided to sell. In this case the owner was not trying to save taxes. In fact, this owner wasn't even taking a salary, a draw, or getting any real benefit from ownership.

In this case, changes were made to the compensation packages of the nail technicians. Most of the expense of the shop, other than rent, was for payments to the five ladies who were providing the services.

They were on a 60/40 split with the owner getting 40%. In addition, the owner was generously providing medical insurance.

The owner explained to the manicurists that there was no reason to continue in business if there was no income generated for the owner. They agreed to change the split to 50/50, and eliminate the medical insurance (four of the women had insurance through their spouses.)

This resulted in an immediate increase in income from -0- to $80,000 per year and a buyer was found quickly who was willing to pay $85,000 for the company.

Why is it important to make changes to bookkeeping practices and tax strategies two years before you put the company on the market? It should be no surprise that many potential owners will be suspicious of sudden changes in profits just prior to sale. In the case of the nail salon above, the change was very obvious, and the technicians were still on the job, so it wasn't as suspicious.

In many cases, however, the changes are harder to prove. Some companies employ one or more relatives who may be getting paid far more than they are worth. Taking such an employee off the books three months prior to sale will increase profits, but a wary buyer may think that this employee was contributing more than the owner admits.

Increases in margin, lowered losses due to shrink, decreases in advertising or travel expense are all suspect if the changes are only in place for a limited time. The travel and advertising might be necessary to achieve current sales levels. The margins may not be sustainable over time as customers rebel against higher prices.

It may seem Pollyannaish to suggest that the best way to run a business is to maximize profits and pay taxes on those profits without stretching the tax law too far. This will definitely help you sleep better at night. The reality is that most of us are trying too hard to avoid the tax man, and sometimes this is done in ways that actually harm the business. Being forced into a higher tax bracket is a GOOD thing. You only pay more taxes when you earn more money.

A FINAL WORD

You've made it to the end and we are so grateful! We truly hope that you've found one or two pieces of information that can help your business become more profitable with less effort. If those one or two pieces work for you, we encourage you to come back again and again to revisit the concepts and help secure a more thorough understanding.

Businesses continue to grow and thrive only as the owners and managers themselves continue to grow in their knowledge and apply that knowledge towards their efforts.

Good luck!

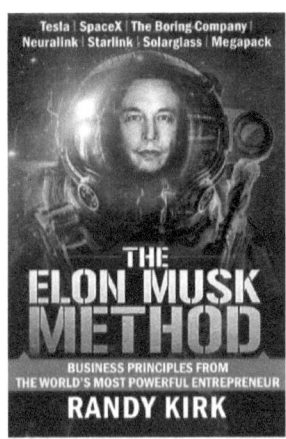

THE ELON MUSK METHOD: *Business Principles from the World's Most Powerful Entrepreneur*

What does Elon Musk know that you don't?

- Elon Musk built Zip2 from a start-up to $22 million paycheck in three years.
- Then Musk built X from a start-up to $160 million paycheck in four years.
- Since then, he has created SpaceX and Tesla giving Musk an estimated net worth of $20 billion.

Would you like to achieve even a fraction of his success? Now you can.

Serial entrepreneur and best-selling author, Randy Kirk, exposes 16 secret principles that guide Elon Musk in his entrepreneurial decisions, including:

- How to become a visionary that profits;
- How to uncover the principles of running a successful business;
- How Elon Musk uses networking to scale his businesses;
- How you should be using your passion and persistence;
- How to maximize the potential of any business regardless of its size;
- The counterintuitive thinking about quality and cost;
- Why *The Elon Musk Method* works to generate successful enterprises of any kind.

WHEN FRIDAY ISN'T PAYDAY: *How to Plan, Start, Build, and Manage Your Small Business*

Are you at a loss with your small business? Founder of 24-plus small businesses, Randy will teach you how to increase sales, hone your marketing, and scale your business to the next level. This comprehensive 400-page book has it all.

There is a right way and wrong way to start a business, and Randy will show you how. Once you get through that, owning and managing a small business is a twenty-four hour a day, seven days a week job. It involves dealing with small and not so small challenges on a daily basis such as planning, marketing, managing, and more. Again, Randy will guide you.

"My favorite section of When Friday Isn't Payday is called 'Dealing with Crisis.' There, Kirk takes a couple of classic small company crises - such as not meeting payroll - and calmly lists possible solutions. This is Kirk at his best, an experienced small business owner figuratively at your side, keeping panic at bay with practical solutions. What separates this book from the pack is relentless practicality." - Inc. Magazine

www.ingramcontent.com/pod-product-compliance
Lightning Source LLC
Chambersburg PA
CBHW020630220526
45464CB00001B/96